Lessons from My Uncle James

Beyond Skin Color to the Content of Our Character

Ward Connerly

ENCOUNTER BOOKS
NEW YORK · LONDON

Published by Encounter Books, an activity of Encounter for Culture and Education, Inc., a nonprofit tax exempt corporation.

Encounter Books website address: www.encounterbooks.com

Manufactured in the United States and printed on acid-free paper.

The paper used in this publication meets the minimum requirements of ANSI/NISO Z39.48-1992 (R 1997) (Permanence of Paper).

Library of Congress Cataloging-in-Publication Data

Connerly, Ward, 1939–
    Lessons from my Uncle James : beyond skin color to the content of our character / Ward Connerly.
      p.   cm.
    ISBN-13: 978-1-59403-221-9 (hardcover : alk. paper)
    ISBN-10: 1-59403-221-1 (hardcover : alk. paper)
    1. Louis, James, 1916–1996. 2. Louis, James, 1916–1996—Philosophy. 3. Connerly, Ward, 1939—Family. 4. Connerly, Ward, 1939—Childhood and youth. 5. African Americans—Biography. 6. African American men—Biography. 7. Uncles—United States—Biography. 8. Conduct of life. 9. Social values—United States. 10. United States—Race relations. I. Title.
    E185.97.L83C66 2008
    979.4'53043092—dc22
    [B]   2008014597

To my cousin Phyllis,
who is like a sister to me.
We were blessed to share in the lives
of James and Bertha Louis.
May the wonderful memories
of their lives, and especially their
good humor, guide us forever!

Contents

Foreword

On August 28, 1963, during the historic March on Washington, one of the most honored figures in American life, Martin Luther King Jr., shared his "dream" that one day his four little children would live in a nation where they would "not be judged by the color of their skin but by the content of their character." Every year, as we celebrate the life of Dr. King, we summon these haunting words as a reminder of the "colorblind" aspiration of most Americans.

I often think, however, that we have ignored the fact that Dr. King's dream was inherently a two-part vision: building a colorblind society, yes, but also developing individuals with good character. Since the murder of Dr. King, our nation has struggled mightily to attain his colorblind vision, but we have often fallen far short of building the kind of individual character that defines a good person.

My friend Harlan Crow, a highly successful businessman, once told me that his greatest wish for his children was that they grow up to be people of good character. When I thought about his comment later on, I thought too of Dr. King's dream and of my Uncle James. These three men on widely divergent life paths all wanted the same thing for their children, and in Uncle James' case for his nephew also: they wanted us to have good character.

It is often said that America is "a nation of immigrants," but I believe this characterization causes us to misplace our focus. America is a nation of individuals. We are a people who have relied heavily on certain fundamental principles and values that have served as the pillars of our society. Our values have guided the development of our culture from our founding; and our principles are greater than our institutions and more critical to social cohesion than our laws. To the extent that all Americans—rich or poor, white or black, Democrat or Republican, from the East or the West—embrace these principles, then do we form a society that is worthy of honor.

After my mother died while I was still a child, I became the responsibility of my maternal grandmother, "Mom," who sent me to live for a period with one of her daughters, Bertha, and Aunt Bert's husband, James Louis. While I am not perfect by any means, the lessons passed on to me by Uncle James have, I believe, served me well. They are lessons that most good parents have passed along to their children. They are lessons that, taken together, have helped build a nation of individuals with good character, a nation that exemplifies the "American character."

Because many of the lessons taught to me by Uncle James have been crucial to my campaign against race, gender and ethnic preferences, I have drawn here on my autobiography, *Creating Equal: My Fight Against Race Preferences*, where I chronicled that campaign. I have also drawn on the love of Uncle James and Aunt Bert and

Mom—all of whom have gone on to their final rest. I wish it were possible for every child to have access to such basic values as the ones they taught.

To Jennifer Bollenbach and Robyn Miller—two fantastic and profoundly dedicated as well as creative staff members—I give my thanks for all your invaluable assistance during the course of this project.

I also offer my profound thanks to Harlan, Kathy and Jack for providing me with the inspiration for this book.

Finally, to the reader, I apologize for the use of a certain four-letter word that often finds its way into the comments of Uncle James. He was a very down-to-earth man who spoke in common terms. To cleanse his language would not present him in an authentic manner. I hope this effort in conveying the real James Louis rather than some sanitized version will not offend.

Lessons from My Uncle James

"**H**ome is the place where, when you have to go there, they have to take you in."

This is one of Robert Frost's best-loved lines—a shrewd comment on the obligations of blood relationships and on the way that DNA, lineage and kinship can make you an automatic stakeholder in a complex web of associations. You are not required to earn the privilege of belonging, Frost says; simply by being born into a set of genetic relationships you're endowed with a "home" where you can always go.

People quote this line so often that it has attained the status of conventional wisdom. Indeed, it's a comforting sentiment—a genteel New England vision of the advantages of the clan, and certainly a far better alternative than the one offered by Frost's contemporary Tennessee Williams, who said that the best we could hope for was the kindness of strangers. But in my own experience as someone who was ejected from his birthright in early infancy and who has seen varieties of emotional homelessness ever since, "home" is not as certain a refuge as Frost suggests. It may be automatic for some, but others have to fight for it, or luck into it. Society no longer expects its members to offer their kin even the wintry generosity that Frost envisions. If they do take you in, it is something of a miracle—in Christian terms, an act of grace.

These thoughts come to me every time I think of my Uncle James—James Louis was his full name—and the gift of life and learning and "home" that he gave me, a gift all the more precious because it was given not as a result of some blood debt but out of the goodness of his heart.

I was five years old when I went to live with Uncle James and Aunt Bert. I had seen James many times when I was younger, but remembered him only as the anonymous figure who had married my mother's sister and taken her to live thousands of miles from us. When I was told one afternoon that I'd be traveling across the country to join his household, I had no idea what to expect, no certainty about what kind of "home" I'd find with him.

When I came into James' custody, moreover, I wasn't much of a bargain—an awkward and uncertain boy, burdened by a tangled family background that was filled with death and abandonment, missing persons and unexplained absences, all of it played out against the sinister backdrop of the segregated South. It would take me half a lifetime to understand the story, and even after I'd gotten the basic chronology straight, parts of it still didn't make sense. But this much was clear: My mother, Grace, a beautiful and warm-hearted woman I know primarily by other people's descriptions and recollections, died in 1943, when I was just four years old, of what people vaguely referred to as a "stroke." My lasting image of her was of a serene face nesting on the silk bedding of the coffin when I was hoisted up for a last goodbye, a moment comprising equal parts of heartbreak and fear.

My mother was still a young woman at her death, but she had already suffered a lifetime's portion of tragedy. Part of it involved a horrific auto accident that left her with a plate in her skull and a body that never really healed. Another part—perhaps a larger part—involved physical as well as psychological abuse, I have been told, at the hands of my father, Roy Connerly. Something of a "fancy man," as wandering husbands were called in those days, he had left her and me when I was still a two-year-old toddler. No, not so much "left" us as *returned* us, like a defective purchase that didn't live up to his expectations.

That event I do remember. Accompanied by a woman named Lucy, who was young enough to be called a girl but already his mistress, he brought my mother and me to my grandmother's house in the small Louisiana town of Leesville one afternoon.

"I'm giving them back to you, Miss Mary," he told her as she opened the front door.

She gave us all a quick once-over to assess the situation.

"Thank you for bringing them," she replied in a frosty imitation of Southern gentility.

My mother and I entered my grandmother's living room, while Roy Connerly turned and, with Lucy in tow, walked down the stairs of the porch and out of my life. A few days later, in an act of chilling finality, my father— my biological father, as I eventually came to think of him—brought my little red wagon by my grandmother's house and left it on the porch without even bothering to knock on the door.

I didn't see Roy Connerly again for over fifty years. Like all semi-orphans, I suppose, I was unconsciously looking for him all that time, although I tried to make contact only once. That was in 1957, when I graduated from high school in Sacramento and applied to American River Junior College, the only school I could afford. I managed to locate my father's address by querying the extended family and sent a letter asking for $35 to purchase a semester's worth of books. I never received an answer.

It wasn't until 1998 that Roy Connerly accidentally re-entered my life. I had been the subject of a profile in the *New York Times* in July 1997. The author, Barry Bearak, asked me about my father while doing his research. My answers to his questions were so vague that I suspect he doubted me when I told him that I didn't know and didn't particularly care whether Roy Connerly was dead or alive.

A few days after the *Times* published his story, Bearak called and asked, somewhat theatrically, "Are you sitting down?"

"Yes," I replied. "What's up?"

"I've located your father," Bearak said. "He's back in Leesville but he doesn't have long to live." Then he asked what I felt upon hearing this information.

"No big deal," I replied.

He asked whether I had any intention of visiting Roy Connerly.

Still trying to digest the news, I said that I didn't know what I would do.

"Well, I'm interested in what you decide," Bearak said, "not so much as a reporter, but because I'd like to see you reach closure on this matter. I can tell that it has haunted you for a long time."

Weeks later, I happened to get an invitation to speak at Tulane University. The day of my talk turned out to be rainy and dreary. When I was done with the event, I decided to rent a car and drive the 250 miles or so from New Orleans through the bayou country of Louisiana back to my old hometown.

On the outskirts of Leesville, I stopped at a pay phone and called the number I had gotten from Bearak. Roy Connerly's wife, a woman named Clementine, answered. I told her who I was and that I had come to visit my father. She responded graciously, telling me to stay put and she would send someone to lead me to the house. The man who appeared turned out to be another of Roy Connerly's sons. He told me that he had another brother, which meant that I had two half-brothers.

When I arrived at the house, I was ushered into a room where a frail, arthritic old man—not the epic figure of my imagination—was lying in what soon became his death bed. I had always imagined that seeing him once again would be one of those literary moments filled with the pathos of might-have-beens, a melodrama of potential reconciliation. But this biological father of mine was at a loss for words and hardly remembered me. I did feel a certain curiosity about the mystery he represented and asked him whether he cared about me at all. As he struggled to comprehend what was happening, other questions came swarming into my mind, but out of the corner of my eye I saw his wife shaking her head in a gesture intended to deter me from pursuing these ghosts.

Our reunion turned out to be flat and prosaic. He was sphinx-like, unable to answer the questions I asked. I couldn't make myself think of him as anything more than a stranger I might have happened to meet once in another life.

The brief encounter ended with impersonality rather than a salving epiphany. At most, I felt a sort of bitter thankfulness that I had been spared the life I would have led if Roy Connerly had not deserted me. I had come to his home with minimal expectations; I left with none at all. His paternity, such as it was, had nothing to say for itself.

A few weeks later I got a call from Roy Connerly's wife informing me that he had died and asking if I would be attending the funeral. I told her that I thought not.

He had washed his hands of me long since, and there was nothing he could have given me in this last visit even if he had wanted to. But I did come away from our first and only meeting in half a century with one valuable insight: I didn't feel particularly unrequited by the lack of any kind of bond between us because I actually had a father during all those years—my Uncle James.

⋇

As I've said, James Louis didn't have to take me into his home. He had no blood obligation to make sure that I survived, let alone that I thrived and became an independent and self-sufficient individual. I was someone else's burden, if you will, and only tenuously connected to him by kinship. Why, then, did James Louis welcome me? For one thing, he had a tender heart, and like many strong men he did not feel weakened by acting on its commands. More significantly, though, he had made a pledge involving me, and keeping it was a matter of honor for him.

Perhaps feeling a premonition of death, my mother had sought out Uncle James and Aunt Bert for a private moment before the two of them left Louisiana for the state of Washington and the freedom of the North in 1943. Using my childhood nickname, she had said to James Louis, "You'll take care of Billy if the time comes." As it has been explained to me since, this was a statement more than a request. James Louis told my mother that he would, and when the time came to keep that promise he didn't hesitate. He was one of those men—increasingly old-fashioned now—for whom his word was his bond. There was no big walking and backfilling, no excuses, no "depends on what you mean by 'is' ...." The importance of keeping your promises, of treating them as something that keeps the world spinning, was a core value for him and one of the many lessons he taught me.

My grandmother, "Mom" to me, had become my official custodian after my mother's death and would be a central presence in my life until her own passing in 1977. But in the year or so I lived with her in Leesville, she became increasingly fearful that some caprice of the system might take me away from her—not an unfounded fear for a single black woman who had spent all her life enmeshed in the sinister Jim Crow rules of the Deep South. In particular, Mom was worried that my father might suddenly appear on the doorstep once again, this time to demand that I be returned to him in an arbitrary exercise of blood rights that some Southern bureaucrat—even more prejudiced against black women than black men—might carelessly affirm. This fear became a fixation with her.

What some of her relatives regarded as paranoia was validated when she was informed by the wife of the local

Leesville banker that Roy Connerly had indeed been seen around town and that he was indeed asking about "how to get his boy back." The banker's wife, a white woman, was a friend of Mom's and was worried that if the matter ever got to court, Roy Connerly might well prevail. She knew that this not only would break Mom's heart but would not be in my best interest. Therefore, it was her strong advice that Mom get me out of town and out of Louisiana.

Mom made a long-distance call to Uncle James and Aunt Bert. At that time, they were living in Bremerton, Washington, where James was doing wartime work at the Puget Sound Naval Shipyard.

"You got to come get Billy," Mom said. "I don't trust this situation. Something bad could happen to him."

James could easily have told her that she was exaggerating the threat from Roy Connerly, whose rumored interest in custody was obviously bluster or perhaps a cynical attempt to manipulate her emotions. But there was the matter of that promise. Thus, when the phone conversation was over, he told Aunt Bert, "You go on down there and get that boy and bring him up here where he'll be safe."

And so in 1944 my aunt traveled back to the segregated world from which she and James had escaped—for good, they thought—a couple of years earlier. She arrived at Mom's house nervous about being back in Louisiana and anxious to leave as soon as possible. I vaguely remember the hushed preparations: making sandwiches for the journey; packing my few possessions, including all my clothing, in one small suitcase. Then the trip to the Greyhound station, with Mom and Aunt Bert looking around warily for someone who might try to stop us at the last minute. And, finally, my aunt and I boarding the bus that served as our family's updated version of the underground railroad, although naturally we went directly to the back seats. The motor of the bus coughed and we were off to Bremerton, with Aunt Bert and me waving at Mom as she receded into the distance.

Looking back on it now, I see this incident as a story not only about finding a home where they don't *have* to take you in, but also about the black family in an era before the word "dysfunctional" had become permanently attached to it. In my time of need, the black family functioned very well indeed. That it no longer does so with predictability for others in situations similar to the one I experienced is a tragedy that ought to concern us all.

My first impression of Bremerton upon arriving there was that I must be in a foreign country. My first impression of Uncle James was that he was somewhat foreign too. He was certainly far blacker than Aunt Bert or me, the depth of pigment giving his skin a permanent sheen. He was not a man to waste words, but he had a hearty laugh that he made no attempt to suppress and a mischievous gleam in his eye that offered a promise of interesting things to come. He carried himself like a free man, which made him unique in my experience of malehood up until then. Even the cockiest of black men in Leesville had seemed to be always looking over their shoulders.

The matter of Uncle James' color was an issue for my mother's side of the family, as indeed it was for everyone in the melanin-crazed South. The Sonieas were light-skinned, their heritage including Cajun and Irish as well as American Indian. (In fact, the family patriarch,

Eli Soniea—a successful carpenter—had "passed for white" in the 1920s.) "High yeller" might have been a term of contempt in the white precincts of Louisiana, but for the Sonieas, who had internalized the caste distinctions of the Deep South as completely as members of the magnolia-scented white aristocracy, these words had a more positive connotation. Being "high yeller" meant they had climbed to a higher rung on the black community's mirror-image social ladder. Some of them clung fiercely to this status primarily to distinguish themselves from those of James Louis's hue. In fact, I later learned that some of the male Sonieas—my mother's brothers— regarded Uncle James as being beneath them and had called him "an ignorant nigger." Such words were uttered only behind his back and then with great caution.

If the Sonieas had a documented lineage that could be traced back for several generations, James Louis's genealogy was far thinner. He was born in Natchez, Mississippi, in 1916 to a dirt-poor family of sharecroppers. (His father had been born at the tail end of Reconstruction and went through his life without ever owning any part of the land he worked or the house in which he lived.) As a young man, Uncle James had kicked around the South taking on a variety of odd jobs. He finally settled for a time in New Orleans and was working there as a deck hand on a Mississippi River cargo ship when he was introduced to Aunt Bert by a friend of my mother's. He won Bert's heart by his plucky initiative and his sneaky sense of humor. But Mom didn't allow them to date until James came to the house and formally presented himself for her inspection as a serious suitor. When he did this, she sensed immediately that he was good-humored, dependable and ambitious, not only for worldly goods but for a better, freer life, and she quickly gave the courtship her blessing.

That was just before Pearl Harbor. When the war came, James saw an opportunity finally to escape the world of segregation once and for all, while also doing something for the war effort. (He was too old to enlist.) So he applied for work at the Puget Sound Naval Shipyard. I was later told that he regarded the letter offering him a job as his own personal emancipation proclamation.

Even though I shared the Soniea bloodline and physical appearance, James seemed to me a far more striking figure than any of those high yeller uncles I had known in my early years back in Leesville. Six feet tall and powerfully built, his dark skin setting off the whiteness of his teeth, he was a good-looking man who, judging from his facial features, probably had some distant American Indian ancestry himself. But Uncle James was not interested in talk of blood quantum and racial classification; and when his in-laws spoke about such things, his face went blank with boredom, like a television set that has just been switched off. He felt that people's color was the least interesting fact about them, and, as for himself, he didn't care where he had come from, only where he was going. The only thing he wanted from the world was for it to respect him and regard him as a man—a word he pronounced, in the down-home accent he never quite lost, as "mane."

Uncle James was capable of deep sentiment, but he kept it buried under a thick layer of pragmatism. He had a somewhat gruff manner, but it was always subverted by a broad grin that he couldn't suppress. He was fundamentally a cheerful man, for whom optimism was a worldview as well as a strategy for daily life. "You're going to catch a whole lot more flies with honey than with vinegar" was one of a handful of maxims by which he charted his life. He valued humility and didn't like people who took themselves and their opinions too seriously.

James was not the sort of man to dandle a boy affectionately on his knee or to commiserate with him on the psychological trauma he might have experienced because of the loss of a mother and rejection by a father. Although I deeply desired to be comforted for these losses when I first arrived in James Louis's household, I soon understood that he would not requite me. His idea, from the moment I stepped foot in the living room of the Bremerton house, was that I should stand on my own two feet. His message was unequivocal: "You stop your complaining, hear! Take charge of your life right now, boy!"

I got that message and saw its value. But I also got another message as well, one that was more subliminal. James made it clear from the day I arrived that I was valued, and, even more importantly, that I would be protected for the first time in my life. I knew without his ever saying a word that James had taken responsibility for me and would never let anything bad happen. Over time, I gradually came to accept this feeling as normal. There were no contingencies to my membership in his household, no sense that he was doing me a favor and that some lapse on my part might imperil the relationship. James never pretended that I was not another man's son, but he made it clear from the beginning that I was part of *his* family. As I think back on how he treated me, I understand why Justice Clarence Thomas wrote in his autobiography about being his "grandfather's son."

The similarities between my uncle and Thomas's grandfather are striking.

If the major division in the black community during the twentieth century was between the vision of Booker T. Washington (who urged blacks to make a place for themselves in America by working patiently for incremental change through "constructive action") and that of W. E. B. Du Bois (who thought black people's best hope for advancement was through the efforts of an elite rather than the labors of the common man, and who believed that American racism was perdurable), I suppose that James had to be counted as an unabashed Washingtonian. He didn't look to black intellectuals to tell him what to do. Early in his life he had decided to avail himself of the benefits that came from heeding Booker T.'s injunction to American blacks to "cast down your bucket where you are." He believed in the American Dream and believed too that he could use sweat equity to get fractional ownership in it. He always felt that as a result of having cast down his own bucket he had pulled up a good life.

In the late 1990s, after James Louis was gone, I was once invited to give a talk on race at Harvard University. After I had finished, several people gathered around to continue the discussion. One of them introduced himself as the great-grandson of Booker T. Washington. He said he felt that his ancestor had been "smeared" as an Uncle Tom by black radicals but would be vindicated by history. Then he said, "Your message against race preferences is essentially the same as my grandfather's— we need to stand on our own two feet, rely on ourselves and stop blaming the world for our problems. I believe you'll be vindicated too." I was struck by the fact that all of the Bookerite ideas he had attributed to me had come directly from my Uncle James.

During the couple of years that we lived in Bremerton, James did well. I did too, starting school and beginning to make friends. But by 1947, the shipbuilding business was slumping in the postwar military build-down. Along with countless others looking for a place to cast down their next bucket, James focused on California. He had heard that this was the place where the future was being born, so he decided to move us there. He picked Sacramento because of good reports he had heard about it from former co-workers in the shipyards who had left for its greener pastures. So, one day, he packed Aunt Bert and me and all our belongings into the car and a trailer, and made the long drive through southern Washington, Oregon and northern California to a Sacramento neighborhood called Del Paso Heights. James put a down payment on a small and tidy house and began looking for work.

Once a vast section of cropland that had become a giant housing development a generation earlier, "the Heights," as we soon called it, was neatly divided into black and white sections, with Rio Linda Boulevard as the dividing line. But the street was not the tracks and there was no other side. It was custom, not law, that kept the races separate in the Heights; and this made the separation feel more like choice than compulsion. None of Del Paso Heights' white or black citizens worried much about what might happen if they strayed to the other side of Rio Linda Boulevard.

Like other recent immigrants, James and Aunt Bert were soon spreading the good news about the land of milk and honey to family and friends back in Louisiana.

My grandmother responded by moving to Sacramento too, living first with her oldest daughter, Cleo, and then buying a vacant lot a few blocks away from us where she planned eventually to build a small house. Then came a gradual immigration of the extended family of Sonieas, ultimately transforming our neighborhood into a sort of Louisiana-in-California.

A couple of my aunts became maids in William Land Park, a large middle-class housing development in east Sacramento. They were glad for the work and not in the least resentful of tending to white folks. They felt that having arrived in California they were halfway to what Dr. King called the "Promised Land" and if they worked hard their children at least would complete the journey. They were on the same wavelength as James, who once said to me (in colorful language these aunts would not have approved of), "I'll shovel shit all my life if that means that you won't have to shovel shit at all."

⸻◈⸻

Still my legal guardian, Mom, who could finally believe that the threat of Roy Connerly was gone forever, demanded that I now come and live with her. I resisted as long and as hard as I could, and so did Uncle James. He and Bert had produced their own child, my cousin Phyllis, in 1950, and he believed I was part of his brood. But Mom had made up her mind and there was no changing it. She came to James' house one day when he was at work and told me to gather up my clothes and other possessions and then dragged me crying to her place.

"Where's Wardell?" James asked when he got home.

"Mama came and got him today," Bert timorously replied.

"I'm going to go get him and bring him back."

But when James reached the front door, Bert stopped him. He paused, turned around and studied the look on her face for a moment, and then returned to the living room.

"It's just not right," Aunt Bert later told me he kept muttering as he wandered through the house that evening.

The law was on Mom's side, and in any case he didn't want to risk a family fight by challenging her. But the transition turned out to be less drastic than any of us imagined. I might now be living under Mom's roof, but I was still in some sense a part of the James Louis household. He lived minutes away; his house was still my house. His interest in me did not diminish, nor did his intention to be my model and teacher as well as my protector. In this last role he was ever vigilant.

Mom had managed to get a loan of $3,500 to build a permanent home on her vacant lot. As part of the cost-cutting deal she made with the contractor she hired, I was volunteered as an unpaid laborer. After school and on weekends I cleaned up the job site, straightened bent nails so they could be reused, and did other menial jobs.

After several weeks I was feeling ground down, and I got permission, or so I thought, to knock off after working half a Saturday so I could join some friends who were going to the movies—one of those Republic Studio cowboy movies, as I recall, that showed at the local theater along with serials and cartoons on Saturday afternoons. (I was addicted to heroes such as Gene Autry, Tom Mix, Lash LaRue, and especially the Lone Ranger. I wanted to be cool and controlled like him, although I knew that I probably looked more like Tonto.)

But a problem arose when my Uncle William, a son of Mom's and one of those "high yeller" Sonieas who secretly scorned Uncle James, appeared on the construction site, having appointed himself supervisor for a day. As I was trying to finish up, he told me that I would have to stay on the job for the rest of the afternoon even though the contractor himself had released me. My heart sank. I had resigned myself to missing the cowboy movie when James drove up.

He slowly got out of the car and walked around the new building with his hands in his pockets, evaluating the progress the contractor was making. Then he moseyed over to where I was miserably picking up lumber scraps.

"I thought you were going to the picture show today," he said laconically after watching me for a short while.

I told him that I had been ordered to stay and work.

James pondered the situation a moment or two, and then sauntered over to where Uncle William was standing.

"That boy is going to the pictures," he said, gesturing at me with his head.

William started to bluster.

"Naw, I said the boy's going to the picture show," James repeated, raising his voice a notch. "He worked in school all week and now worked out here most of the morning."

William again started to assert his authority, but James cut him off once and for all: "I'm telling him to go and if you don't like it, then let's you and me settle it."

William took one look at James and wisely decided not to pursue the matter any further. Formally released, I ran off to be with my friends at the movies, feeling as though I'd made a prison break.

Being a dedicated observer of Uncle James, especially during my teen years, I was struck with particular force by two characteristics of his. One was his uncompromising moral code. Most of the adults I knew talked a good game of morality, but when it came right down to cases they practiced what might be called situational ethics. Not James. When he told me never to take anything that didn't belong to me, for instance, he meant exactly what he said. He wouldn't pick up a penny on the street without worrying that it belonged to someone nearby who had just dropped it. He always carefully counted out the change he received at a store, less to make sure he had gotten what he had coming than out of concern that a clerk might inadvertently have given him too much.

To this day, I find myself counting the change given back to me in a retail transaction to make sure that the cashier didn't shortchange herself. I recall the look of shock when I called a cashier's attention to the fact that she had given me too much. I had purchased an item that cost $6.42. I gave her a $10 bill. But instead of giving me $3.58, she gave me $6.42. We argued for three or four minutes before I was able to convince her that she had given me the amount of the purchase rather than the difference between the purchase and the $10 that I had given her.

The other thing I noticed about James was that he drove himself hard and yet never felt any of the "stress" we today tend to associate with strenuous effort. Far from it, James always made it clear that work was more than livelihood for him; it was a life principle. In his off hours he was always sharpening, painting, repairing, polishing, mowing. He put everything into his labor, paid and unpaid, letting himself be defined by it. And he did it all with monumental good humor.

Somewhere in my reading I once came across an aphorism that I've never forgotten: "If I should cease to work, my worlds would tumble." This thought fit James exactly. Work was not only self-definition, but also a way of keeping the chaotic forces of life at bay.

Not long after we moved to California, James got a job at a sawmill in a place called Oregon House, a little company-owned town just outside the city of Grass Valley, in the low sierra of the California Gold Country about fifty miles north of Sacramento. I tagged along with him during summer vacations. We would leave Sacramento on Sunday afternoon in James' old Model A so we could get set up to work first thing the next morning. Aunt Bert always packed us a lunch (James called it "dinner") that we ate on the way.

During the two-hour drive to Oregon House, we listened to country music and James presented me with a philosophy of life, whose major themes had to do with pride and personal responsibility. The last item was of particular concern to James. He always said you could tell a responsible person by whether he shined his shoes, took care of his car, cut the grass, and looked after his dog. Contrary to the currently fashionable view, Uncle James believed that you *should* sweat the small stuff, because if you did that, the big stuff would fall into place by itself.

I can still see him standing on top of those ten-foot lumber piles up at Oregon House, wrestling the thick 2x12 lumber, which was still "green" and heavy with moisture, into piles. He is wearing heavy overalls, in the middle of summer, to protect against splinters from the green lumber. The sweat is pouring off him, making his dark skin gleam even more than usual. He has a big grin on his face as he pauses for a moment to pull a red bandana out of his back pocket and mop his forehead. He is a figure of power and confidence, and he embodies what the great black writer Ralph Ellison once called "heroic optimism": the belief that a combination of effort and endurance— along with the ultimate goodness of this country, whatever its past sins—would bring us all through.

After the Oregon House mill closed down, Uncle James went to work for the Teichert Company, a construction firm in Sacramento, and continued there for almost thirty years until his retirement in 1981. All this time, even when he was well into his sixties, he trenched foundations and did other hard labor in the housing developments in which Teichert built the infrastructure throughout the Sacramento area. Not only did he work hard himself, but he functioned as a sort of whip for other employees, urging them by his example to put out an honest day's work for an honest day's pay. James did this not because he was trying to curry favor with his employer—although there was often something extra in his envelope on pay day—but rather because for him hard work was simply a moral principle.

Uncle James' attitude toward hard work is probably responsible for the fact that I don't believe in the concept of "retirement." In my view, as long as you are healthy, no matter how many years you have lived, you should try to be productive in your society. For me, this means going into the office or writing a column or doing something to stay active. "Retiring" is not my cup of tea. We are too anxious to ship individuals who are capable of being productive out to pasture just because they reach some magical point on the time line.

In his later years, when he was able to enjoy a comfortable retirement as a result of a lifetime of thrift, I think James took some satisfaction in seeing that his preaching on the gospel of hard work had taken hold with me. I don't mean that he lived vicariously through what I achieved; Uncle James' own life—even when it slowed down—was always too rich and rewarding for that. But I think he had always regarded me as something of a "project" and saw what I accomplished as a sort of yardstick that measured how far he had come and how far he had brought us all during his lifetime. Barely literate himself, James Louis was proud when I became the first of the family to graduate from college; always an employee himself, he was proud when I started a business of my own.

Shortly after I purchased an old Victorian as an office building to house Connerly & Associates, a housing and land use consultancy that my wife, Ilene, and I began, Uncle James came for a visit. I gave him a tour of the building and then we went outside. A look of pure joy came over James' face as we stood by the apricot tree in the back yard. His surrogate son owned a business and even an office building! But, as always, he wanted to make sure that I didn't forget where we had come from. "Always be good to your workers and they'll be good to you," he said. I didn't really have many workers, at least not yet, but I knew exactly what he meant. He had said it in another way many times during my growing up: Don't get too big for your britches.

Uncle James was particularly proud when I was appointed to the University of California Board of

Regents. I think he was proudest of all when I got involved in Proposition 209, the measure that ultimately ended race preferences in the state of California.

Looking back on it, I realize now that it was only natural that this measure should have appealed to him. Its central principle—that the state should not discriminate against people on the basis of color, sex or ethnicity, nor award them racial preferences because of these factors— was, in some sense, a vindication of his own approach to life. He had escaped from one social system that made exactly such invidious distinctions between its citizens based on the color of their skin: the system of the Jim Crow South. Freed from this government-mandated discrimination, he had made a good life for himself. Rather than accepting crumbs from the table of some racial bureaucracy, he had risen through the sweat of his brow. He never had to wonder if what he had achieved came because he happened to be a member of a certain race or if his gain had come at the price of someone else's loss.

James Louis believed that there was something wrong with the whole system of race preferences, something desperately at odds with his hero Martin Luther King's vision of a colorblind world where character was more important than skin pigment. First, he resented the system of racial hyphenation upon which preferences must rely. His anger was evident whenever he was watching television and saw someone describe himself as an "African American." He would respond, "Shit, I bet he's never been to Africa and ain't about to go. Those Africans don't want nothing to do with him."

And he resented "affirmative action" because he felt it was a synonym for "handout." When the subject came up, he'd say: "If they got up off their butts and worked, they wouldn't need no affirmative action."

I laughed at his tirades and played the devil's advocate: "But the playing field isn't level for blacks."

"So what," he'd say. "I don't know what playing field you're talking about, but things ain't never going to be equal for everybody. Blacks, whites, whoever—life's not fair whatever your color. Just get out there and do your best at whatever you do and you'll be all right."

We were sitting on the couch one Sunday evening watching a tape of a debate in which I had participated. My opponent had argued forcefully that society wasn't fair to "people of color" and that minorities should be given affirmative action to level the playing field. Uncle James was livid. "You should have told her that nobody gives you shit in life; you got to earn it the hard way."

Even if he might not have been able to wrap the insight in high-flown language, James saw clearly that the end to racial division went not through the pages of the affirmative action handbook, but through the human heart. He was amused when, during the Proposition 209 campaign, I was interviewed on *60 Minutes* by Mike Wallace, who seemed to have trouble believing that race was not a big issue for my wife, Ilene, who is white, and me, nor for our two "mixed race" children, one of whom has scrambled the bloodline even further by marrying a half-Vietnamese woman and having two children with her. I told Wallace that the central question for my kids (and this was another lesson I had learned from my Uncle James) had always been not *what* you are, but *who*.

In late 1995 and early 1996, I often dropped by the home in Rio Linda where Uncle James and Aunt Bert had by then moved from Del Paso Heights. The 209 campaign was just beginning and my purpose in telling James what was happening was to gauge by his reactions if I was on the right track. He was eighty years old, suffering from kidney failure, heart trouble and diabetes, his condition perhaps aggravated by having been exposed to asbestos while working in the shipyards. But he was relentlessly upbeat and interested in the social drama I'd gotten into with the 209 initiative.

He was usually waiting at the dining room window and would come out to meet me as soon as I pulled up. He'd make sure that my car was clean and check out my shoes to see if they were shined. Then he'd come and stand next to me and sidle up to the subject of politics by asking how things were going in "the political world."

He may not have understood all the intricacies of Proposition 209, but he was clear on the core issues because they were also at the core of his life: the importance of earning respect and not taking handouts; of knowing that your achievements are really yours because you've earned them by your sweat rather than having them given to you by someone who demands that you accept victimhood as part of the bargain. It made his blood boil when he heard that some black leaders were calling me a "race traitor" and an "Uncle Tom." There would have been hell to pay if he were a younger man.

"You're right on this, Wardell," he would always say in winding up our conversations about the initiative against racial preferences. "And I don't want you backing down, hear?"

As he exhorted me to continue the fight, despite the attacks being leveled against me by some black people, Uncle James would become irate. In his always-colorful language, which had developed some new shades as he grew older, he would say, "Shit, them people don't know what they're talking about. And anyhow, I didn't raise you to run away from a fight."

James Louis died of kidney failure that spring, a few months before Proposition 209 passed in a landslide vote in California. News that he was gone stopped me in my tracks. My heart felt as though it had been pulled up by the roots. When I spoke at his funeral the words came from my deepest reaches: "I never told you how much I loved you. You weren't educated but you made sure I was. You didn't father me, but you became my father."

That was so: James Louis raised and nurtured me. But he also shaped me in the way that fathers tend to do: by acting as my breakwater against mortality; by doing the right thing when no one was looking (in Bill Bennett's famous definition of character); by providing inconspicuous lessons day in and day out whose cumulative effect over the years was that of a curriculum on how to live with decency and purpose.

And what he taught has stayed with me all the years since—both in my private life, where my goal has been simply to be half as good a man as he was; and in my public life as well, where I have spent more than a decade fighting race preferences all the way from California to Washington and Florida and Michigan and now, in 2008, to Arizona, Colorado, Missouri, Nebraska and Oklahoma.

Not long ago I had a conversation with Justice Clarence Thomas in which I talked a little about Uncle James and the moral curriculum he had set for me in the school of our relationship. Justice Thomas nodded and mentioned his grandfather: "I was raised that way too."

Then, as I described the five-state "Super Tuesday on Race Preferences," he said something that might just as easily have come from Uncle James himself: "You hang tough on this. You stay in there. This is about freedom."

As recently as the 1990s, our society seemed to be getting ever more deeply mired in the politics of race. Affirmative action is still with us, but with each passing day it seems to resemble more and more the appendix of the body politic, a vestigial reminder of a color-coded past. It was always a flawed idea, one whose time as a public policy for a dynamic society probably should never have come and now has clearly gone. America seems at last to be looking ahead to a future of opportunity rather than backward to a past of paralyzing guilt with no chance of redemption. The idea of someone like Senator Barack Obama, who rose on the basis of his own undeniable merits, needing affirmative action reveals the almost comic bankruptcy of this concept in today's social context.

But as we at last seem to be "getting beyond race," we face a dilemma. If, as Martin Luther King "dreamed" in his great 1963 speech at the Washington Monument, the color of our skin seems to matter less with each passing day, the content of our character must necessarily become ever more important. The more we see ourselves as individuals rather than as members of some racial or ethnic group struggling for advantage in a zero-sum political game, the more we must think about the moral guidelines we use in building our individual lives. Character is something we have ignored at our peril for a long time, while we have focused so intently on the matter of race. Now we must bring character back into view as we learn to stop arranging our social life by unjust racial formulae.

Harlan and Kathy Crow are a successful and attractive couple and close friends of mine. A couple of years back, I spent an evening in their home. Over a dinner of fried chicken and mashed potatoes, Harlan introduced me to his son Jack and asked me to spend a few minutes talking to him about the topic of race. This I did, and was surprised at how keen this eleven-year-old's insights about this subject already were. The next day, Harlan gave me a ride to the meeting I was having with Boone Pickens. As we left for Boone's office, Harlan thanked me for the conversation I'd had with his son and said something that made a strong impression on me: "The most important thing I want for Jack and all my kids is that they have good character."

Harlan's wish for his boy was exactly what James Louis had wanted for me—although the two men were worlds apart in other respects. What they both wanted was something that Harlan, with all his resources, could not buy, and that James, with no assets to speak of, knew how to cultivate from within.

How do we begin to make character part of our social world once again? What are its building blocks? How can they be arranged to build a moral life?

When I think about these questions, I think about the lessons my Uncle James taught me and wonder if what this simple but profound man believed—always expressed in the most down-to-earth terms—might not be the starting point for a discussion this country desperately needs to have. James stood for manliness, religion, hard work, personal loyalty and other virtues we now regard as old-fashioned. We have been told that such concepts are obsolete in our postmodern world. I don't think so. I think, in fact, that a case might be made that we must go back to the future to recover these concepts if our broken social world is to work once again.

"A *mane* ain't nothing but a *mane*."

A Lesson about Manhood

James Louis was something of a crossover artist in terms of musical taste. He loved country and western music, regarding it as the common man's guide to pride in country, betrayal in love, the caprice of fate, and other such subjects. But like most black men of his era, Uncle James especially loved the blues. This music tapped into some deep reservoir of pain and longing—but never self-pity—that he kept hidden from the world. His idea about a man being "nothing but a *mane*" must have originated in some blues riff that he once heard.

For James, the phrase contained many messages: that regardless of the accidental inequities of wealth and status, we all face the same bedrock challenges and will be judged on how well or poorly we handle them; that if we are stripped of all our other worldly possessions, we can still make it as long as we retain our individual integrity; and that bravery is the best revenge. I'm sure James didn't know who Aristotle was, but he certainly would have agreed with the great philosopher that courage was the chief of all virtues, because without it all the others are inoperative.

Although he never got past the third grade, Uncle James could read people as well as more formally educated people read books. He was easygoing and loved to joke and kid around, yet he knew that for some people humor could be a sharp instrument used primarily to wound. He was not inclined to be on the receiving end of such humor. Nor was he particularly interested in drawing lines, but if others stepped over one that was obviously there, he immediately called them out. I remember once when my Uncle William lightly called Uncle James "a dumb son of a bitch" in the course of some casual conversation. The comment was delivered with enough ambiguity that it could have been interpreted as a harmless jocularity from one distant relative to another, but Uncle James, possibly knowing that his in-laws looked down on him and considered his blackness a symbol of ignorance, immediately jumped to his feet ready to rumble: "You ever say that again and I'll kick your ass." Uncle William never did. He was slightly bigger, but he knew better than to tangle with Uncle James.

As part of his readiness to stand up and be counted, James Louis "packed heat," as he sometimes called owning and occasionally carrying firearms. I'm sure that the intricate debates over the Second Amendment went right over his head, but he was unshakable in his conviction that he had a right to protect himself, his family and his property, and moreover that the buck for doing this stopped with him. He had guns in all the years that I knew him—rifles and shotguns for hunting and pistols for personal safety. This was not only a right, as he saw it, but an obligation. A *mane* wasn't impetuous, but he didn't allow himself to become a statistic or squander an opportunity for justice by waiting for the police to arrive or for a warrant or a court date. A *mane* took care of his own business whenever he could. Such a conviction was James' way of asserting a vision of a just world. Having come of age in a land of nightriders and Klansmen, he had decided that neither he nor his family would ever again be forced to submit to terror if he could help it.

In our early days in postwar Sacramento, our neighborhoods were relatively clean and safe. But by the late 1960s, as drugs and other vices settled into the black community, this sense of stability began to disappear. James was disturbed by the social turbulence of this period and by its growing amorality. This was not nostalgia for some imagined golden time, but an intuitive understanding that the rug of social cohesion had suddenly been pulled out from under all of us. James often noted with a kind of despair that the menace which in his Louisiana past had come from the white world now came from a growing black subculture of criminality—the self-styled ghetto strongmen who increasingly preyed upon the weak among us. He talked about how, in an escalating redefinition of what constituted serious crime, armed robbery had replaced petty theft and senseless killings had replaced corner shakedowns. It was a world turned upside down—the kind of changes occurring in a few short years that typically take generations to transpire, making individuals like himself feel like exiles in their own lives.

The most colorblind man I ever knew, James wouldn't buy any of the trendy defenses that were offered, primarily by white liberals, to explain—that is, explain *away*—the behavior of the new black predators: that they had been driven mad by white racism; that their violence actually represented "rebellion" rather than sordid criminality. Such notions might have traction in the faculty lounges of the university, but James had a word for them: "bullshit." To him, the black gangsters who had arrived on the scene to prey upon the old, the sick and the weak in our community were simply "bad men." And those who apologized for them in any way were definitely part of the problem rather than part of the solution.

In addition to the pistol he kept near the bed, James sometimes carried one in the car as this epidemic of crime spread into what had always been the civilized parts of our world. When some young gang-banger would get too close, James would give him the evil eye and mutter, "No, you better not come over here. We're packing heat in this car. You don't want a piece of this, that's for sure."

Would James ever have used a weapon? For all his basic humanity, I think the answer is yes. On the one hand, he knew himself well enough to understand that an act of violence that took or jeopardized another life, even if justified in the eyes of the law, would haunt him for the rest of his life. But the people he loved came first. If he had run out of alternatives, James would not have hesitated to take that gun out of the glove box and use it to protect himself and the rest of us.

"Packing heat" may have been more a symbolic state-ment about his unwillingness to become a statistic than anything else, but the sullen corner boys and hard cases who began to appear in our area seemed to sense that James meant business and gave him a wide berth. Even well into his late seventies, white-haired and slowed a lit-tle by having lived a hard life, he still carried himself with authority. Unwilling to become a victim, he was never victimized.

When I think about how important it was to James to be a *mane,* I remember two incidents in particular. The first one occurred one night not long after I had come to live with him and Aunt Bert in Bremerton. She always drove James to work, and then she and I picked him up when his shift at the shipyard was over. On this particular evening he was standing on the curb waiting for us with his empty lunch pail and his usual look of satisfaction at having earned an honest day's pay for an honest day's work. But just as he was about to step into the car, a couple of young white guys sauntered by. One of them made an unintelligible but clearly disparaging remark. Worse yet, he then banged menacingly on the hood of the car. That sent Uncle James over the edge. People might insult him, but nobody touched his car!

I don't know if he was packing heat that night. But if he was, he decided on a graduated response. He immediately flung open the car door and grabbed a snow chain that he kept under the front seat on the driver's side. Swinging it like a cowboy lariat, he ran toward the white boys, who seemed paralyzed by his swift reaction. James may have barely clipped them a couple of times, I'm not sure, but the next thing I knew, they were cowering on the ground begging for forgiveness and he was standing over them with the chain dangling down menacingly. Then he moved away and let them get up and run off. He got back in the car and said, more to himself than to me and Aunt Bert, "I bet you by God they don't mess with me again."

It took Aunt Bert several minutes to compose herself on the way home. Finally, she said reproachfully: "James, you could have gotten us all killed!"

He shook his head stubbornly. "I'm not going to let that trash mess with me. A *mane* has got to defend himself and his family, else he ain't no kind of *mane* at all!"

The second incident came nearly a decade later, in 1950, when James' father died and the three of us drove to Natchez for the funeral. There was no marker at the state line, but we knew when we had passed into Mississippi; the atmosphere of Jim Crow was suddenly as suffocating as the weather. James and Bert became edgy, vigilant. I was just eleven, but they didn't have to tell me that they were recapitulating half a lifetime of second-class citizenship. The structure that had forced this status on them was still standing and now they were back under its control. We traveled carefully, watching where we ate, where we slept, where we relieved ourselves. For me, it was a history lesson that didn't need words.

At one point we pulled into a small country filling station to refuel. It had those old-fashioned pumps where you could see the gas boil up in a large glass cylinder as it entered your tank. A young white attendant who couldn't have been more than sixteen came out of a hut and walked sullenly to the car. He looked down at James through the window and said, "Whatchu want, boy?"

That word "boy" caused a sharp intake of breath on Aunt Bert's part; James flinched as if slapped. He tensed, staring at the white kid for a moment and checking out a couple of older white men who were also on the scene, regarding us indolently from chairs tilted back against the hut. Then James slowly turned toward me and Bert. A look of savage resignation passed over his face. Stonily, he turned back to the attendant and said with clenched politeness, "Fill her up, please, sir."

When we were back on the road, he began to rage: "That little snot-nosed piece of trash! I'd give everything in my pocket to get a chance to kick his ass. He called me *boy!* How old do I have to be before some little son of a bitch like that stops calling me boy? He'd best be thankful that the two of you were in this car."

In retrospect, however, I think James' outburst may have had something to do with his fear that I might think the less of him for not staging a confrontation. But as young as I was and as accustomed as we were to relaxed California attitudes toward race, I knew at the time that his response was a calculated one based on a reckoning of the odds he faced and his certain knowledge that Aunt Bert and I could have been collateral damage of any impetuous act on his part. (This, after all, was not long before the Emmett Till lynching, and black adults—not to speak of teenagers—had to be wary lest a careless remark lead them to become "strange fruit" hanging from Southern trees.) Rather than scorn him for keeping his cool, I appreciated the fact that James had kept the situation from getting out of control. I understood that knowing when to stand down was as much a part of being a *mane* as knowing when to step up; these were two sides of the same coin.

I learned from watching James, and I also learned from listening to him. He never engaged in windy speeches, and he was not inclined to self-dramatization. But from the moment I came under his influence, he made it clear to me, in dozens of small ways and some large ways, that I had to defend myself and, even more importantly, defend my beliefs. I still remember the time when I was nine or ten and got into my first playground rumble. I didn't acquit myself very well. After receiving a pummeling, I dragged myself home disheveled and a bit banged up, manufacturing self-pitying excuses for my poor showing. James caught sight of me as I walked up the driveway, and he came out onto the front porch to meet me. I blurted out what I thought was an affecting account of what had happened to me, while he listened to my tale with a look of rising annoyance.

"I don't want to hear none of this baby stuff, Wardell," he finally interrupted. "Just cut it out cause I don't want to hear it." Then he moved closer so that he could poke his index finger into my chest for emphasis. "I want you to understand me. You don't fight back next time this happens and you're going to get two ass-kickings—the one you get at school and the one you get from me when you come home. And the one you get at home will be worse than the one at school."

These were conventional sentiments of the day—a time before sensitive manhood and conflict resolution scenarios became part of our culture. James was certainly not alone in issuing such warnings; I'm sure many fathers said the same thing. But that was the point: he was acting as my father and taking steps to make sure I survived not only the bullies of the schoolyard but those lying in wait at other venues as well. He didn't necessarily want me to fight, but he did want me to fight *back*.

Soon after we moved to Sacramento, there was another summary moment, this time involving a white girl named Mildred Tittle. I had met her when I was being intimidated by a white man on my way to school one morning. I had picked up walnuts that had dropped from his tree into the street. As he berated me, Mildred came to my defense.

We soon became friends and walked home from school together. It was a little dangerous. At one point, a white kid called her a "nigger lover." But there was racism on the other side too. One day when we were walking home, a couple of very large black girls followed us. After uttering insults under their breath for a block or two, one of them sprang forward and violently yanked Mildred's pigtails to punish her for crossing some imaginary color line. I turned and shoved the girl.

That night, Mom paid me a visit at Uncle James' house, where I happened to be living at the time. She told me that the father of the girl I had shoved, a deacon in our church, had come to see her that evening and complained about me. Pushing his daughter was just one of the charges he had lodged against me; even worse was taking the side of a white girl.

Mom was prepared to punish me because I had made her lose face with a fellow churchgoer and even more because I had broken her cardinal rule about hurting a girl. I explained the circumstances of what had happened and how Mildred had defended me when I needed help; that she was my best friend and had been unjustly picked on. My speech didn't do much to mollify Mom, but James, who had been watching from the background, spoke up: "Miss Mary, I agree with you about boys not hitting girls. But it sounds to me like Wardell did the right thing. That girl had it coming. And her father bringing color into it just isn't right."

Mom thought about it for a minute and then nodded her head. The next day, she and I paid the deacon a visit and she told him in no uncertain terms that the jury had come back with its verdict. I was innocent. And his daughter had better stop picking on that white girl!

Like most people, I've run into tough situations throughout my life—but nothing like what I've experienced in the last fifteen years or so during my campaign against race preferences. There have been anonymous death threats. I have been called every name in the progressive book—Race Traitor, House Nigger, Uncle Tom, Oreo. I have appeared before hostile crowds, primarily on college campuses whose administrators didn't bother to provide security for my appearances, where things could easily have spun out of control. But in these situations I've always looked at myself through James Louis's eyes to make sure that on the one hand I didn't act rashly, but on the other that I wasn't backing down from a fight worth having. I've always felt him there beside me, promising that second ass-kicking if I didn't stand up for myself and the causes I espoused; urging me to try to find the justice of a situation; and reminding me that when push comes to shove, sometimes you can't count on social structures or law enforcement. There's only you and the voice inside. And if you want to be a *mane,* you had better listen hard to this voice and be true to its commands.

"Don't stand there waiting for somebody to give you something."

A Lesson about Work

W hen I was a teenager, my grandmother would sometimes look at me critically while I was sitting around conspicuously doing nothing and say, "You know that idle hands are the devil's workshop, don't you?"

Mom was a deeply and fundamentally religious woman. Those liberal theological precepts which hold that evil is merely the absence of good were not for her. She believed that Satan was an active principle in the world, walking among us and waiting for an opportunity to take advantage of our manifold weaknesses. The Evil One was especially interested in setting snares for young men with empty minds and time on their hands.

Uncle James would not have argued the theology, but he had a less urgent view of the world, believing that people had both good and bad in them and only the Lord (who in any case had Satan under his thumb) knew who was what. He would have agreed with Mom about the dangers of indolence, though. But while she worried that it led to sin, James was bothered by the fact that it led to missed opportunities to "earn your keep." More than once during my growing up when I was at a crossroads with one path leading to self-pitying inaction and the other to hard effort, he told me, "Don't just stand there waiting for someone to give you something." He was a fan of "the purpose-driven life" long before the phrase was coined or the book written.

Someone who didn't really know James Louis might have been tempted to write him off as a sort of black version of Archie Bunker who saw the Seven Deadly Sins (particularly sloth) as dire enemies. It was true that he thought the coffee break was the worst invention in American history. He often commented acidly about people employed by government bureaucracies getting paid with his hard-earned money to "sit on their fat asses smoking cigarettes." Every time he saw young men standing in front of liquor stores and on street corners with signs proclaiming their jive willingness to "work for food," James Louis would mumble to himself, "Well, then, just put down the damned sign and go get yourself a job."

But as I've said, work involved moral principles for him. He strongly believed that not working all-out when you were on the clock was tantamount to theft. His constant counsel to me was: "I don't care if you clean toilets for a living, but if you do, I want you to clean that shit better than anybody in America—and take pride in it."

James was never at rest and he didn't want me to be, either. When he was mowing the lawn or washing the car, I always had a corresponding task to perform—drying the car bumpers to make sure there were no water spots on them, for instance, or sweeping up the lawn clippings that had strayed onto the sidewalk. He was fiercely proud of his house and yard and spent a lot of time on their upkeep. "You got to keep touching home base or you're out of the game," he liked to say.

Whenever he saw me killing time, say, by robotically throwing a baseball against a wall and fielding it on the rebound with my mitt, he would shoot me a disapproving look and say something like, "Boy, make yourself useful." At the time, this injunction was annoying, to put it mildly. I thought James had a problem: the inability to recognize creative leisure when he saw it. Later on, I understood that he wasn't a fan of make-work, or activity for activity's sake. Rather, he was trying to get me to see that a wasted hour is lost forever, and that by constantly working to achieve something, however apparently small, we are arranging the building materials of a productive life.

As I write these words, I realize that it must seem there was something old-fashioned about James' attitude toward work, with its echoes of traditional rugged Americanism and Horatio Alger's can-do optimism. This in fact was the case. James was a throwback, even in his own time. But he knew something in his bones that many of us have forgotten today: work is dignity; work is self-sufficiency; work is independence. James probably didn't know the origin of the now-famous Chinese maxim: Give a man a fish and you feed him for a day; teach him to fish and you feed him forever. But he was certainly familiar with the underlying concept and applied it in his life every day.

Again, it was this lesson that soured me on the concept of retirement. "Senior citizens" also need to feel productive. This is one of the reasons that I applaud the candidacy for president of Senator John McCain. For him, longevity is not a barrier to being of service to his nation.

There is much that I wish I had done better in my life in terms of taking Uncle James' advice, but this lesson of doing for oneself and avoiding dependency is one that I learned early and well.

I remember particularly those summers when I accompanied him to the Oregon House sawmill and watched him work—literally watched, as if he were doing a kind of performance art. They worked in twos at the sawmill, clambering over those giant log piles and trying to cut them down to size. It was hard labor, requiring concentration as well as strength. By the time the sun was at its zenith, James' partner would be begging: "Come on, man. Let's stop and take a break."

"Naw," James would answer as he looked down at me with a wink. "I got to get me some money so I can get that boy there some shoes."

His co-worker would continue to badger him for the next hour or so, and then James would finally shrug with feigned annoyance and say, "Oh, all right. Let's take a minute."

He would dig into his pocket, fish out a dime and toss it down to me. Most of the other workers on the crew, white and black, would do the same. After I had gathered up all the coins, I'd walk to the little company store down the road to get them all Nehi sodas. As I trudged back, I could see that James Louis was getting impatient with the inactivity. After I handed up the sodas, he would tilt his head back and chug down his soda without taking the bottle from his lips, then toss the empty down near where I was standing and immediately get back to work. Again following his lead, the other workers did the same. I gathered up the bottles and took them back to the store. The penny deposit on each of them was mine to keep.

I had to get up at five o'clock every morning while we were at Oregon House, help James cook breakfast, and accompany him to the job site by 6:45. Part of his sales pitch to the supervisor in getting me the job of bottle collector was that empties lying around the site constituted a safety hazard. Having gotten permission for me to be there, he made it very clear to me that he never wanted the "supe" to find any bottles on the ground. But the economic incentive was as persuasive as James' arguments. On a good day I might earn over a dollar, and I was always annoyed when Friday came and stopped my earnings for two days. James would always ask me at the end of his shift, as if I were part of the work gang, "So how much you make today?"

At the end of the workday, I would help him cook dinner on the Coleman stove. After we had eaten, we'd sit outside enjoying the night sounds and the soft twang of country and western songs on the portable radio. Some of the other workers would stroll by and I'd listen in as James talked with them. There were no big subjects, just the easy, meandering talk of men who had put in a good day's work and felt, however intangibly, that by doing this they had also put a small thumbprint on their world.

I have often thought of these men in the years since, particularly when I have heard honest wages degraded as "chump change" and honest work devalued as "slavin' for the man." James Louis would not have put up with such talk. Not for a minute. But more than anything else, I remember the joy of walking between those piles of

lumber and picking up empty bottles and mentally cal-
culating how much I would make when I returned them
to the store. It was this little chore that introduced me to
the world of capitalism and private enterprise.

I learned Uncle James' lessons about work osmotically,
so to speak, internalizing them without knowing that it
was happening. Although we were, in a sense, one big
family, the household that Mom and I inhabited was less
well off than that of James and Bert. At times, the pick-
ins were very slim indeed. I can remember eating a very
skimpy breakfast for several days on end and having din-
ners that consisted of nothing more than a slice of sweet
potato and some collards from our garden.

I knew that Mom had exhausted all her savings in
building our house and still owed on it. She had bor-
rowed from our church's "Poor Folks' Fund" and couldn't
repay the debt with the money she made selling the eggs
from the chickens she raised in our back yard. One day
she came to me and said that our only alternative was to
go on "public assistance," a term she uttered in the same
tone of voice that might have been used for "the peni-
tentiary." But the pill turned out to be even more bitter
than I realized when she first raised the subject. Mom
was not yet sixty-five and did not qualify for Social Security, but at fourteen I was still young enough to qualify
for welfare. So I was the one who would actually have to
sign up for help.

Embarrassed and humiliated, I argued strenuously
against it. But I couldn't deny the dilemma we faced,
since at times I was forced to cut out cardboard insoles
for my only pair of shoes, and I often went without lunch

at school. So eventually I agreed to go down to the Sacramento County office to make a formal application. I still remember that bus ride and how, sitting on the worn seat, I had stared hopelessly out the window at the dull flatness of the passing scenery. It felt as though Novocain had been injected into my spirit. I think in part I was worried about how James would regard me. As it turned out, he knew of the difficulties Mom had faced and had been helping her out here and there. He also knew that I was applying for public assistance, but didn't say anything about it. Afterwards I sometimes wondered if he was purposely standing back, taking a hands-off attitude toward this new development to see how I would handle it.

I qualified for welfare, and for a little over a year we received a monthly payment of $65. This took care of Mom's $35 house payment and left just enough for us to buy food and other necessities. If there had been nothing more to it than opening an envelope every month and cashing the check, I might have been able to regard the $65 as "free money." But luckily there were strings attached that showed what the invisible costs in taking this payment were. Each month we got a visit from a social worker who interviewed us and evaluated how we were using this public assistance, and condescended to us without really meaning to.

I hated these visits more than I can describe. When they were scheduled, I always tried to figure out an excuse to be somewhere else. But since I was technically the one who was the welfare "client," I had to be present. I usually sat there silently staring at the floor during the social worker's interrogation, hating Mom's codependent participation in the bureaucratic routine and sullenly answering questions only when it was impossible not to. I don't know what pushed me over the tipping point, but finally one day I had had enough. With a teenager's impetuous self-righteousness, I suddenly jumped up in the middle of the droning discussion and said that I wouldn't accept another public assistance check. Ever! And the public assistance people shouldn't ever bother to send one because I wouldn't cash it.

The caseworker and Mom both looked at me with disbelief and then shot each other a knowing glance, as if to say that boys would be boys: that it was hormones doing the talking and this bout of teenage histrionics would soon pass. But before they could say anything, I stormed out of the house. I look back on this as the day that I finally became a *mane*.

I went directly to the home of a friend whose father, a man named Lester Brown, was known to be a sort of job broker between Sacramento's downtown Jewish merchants and blacks who did shipping, delivery and other jobs for them. I asked Mr. Brown to help me. He made some calls. As a result, I got a job as a stock boy at the Fabric Center, a downtown furniture store, making 65¢ an hour working after school and on weekends. I put in around twenty-five hours a week and brought home $80 each month. This was more than welfare had given us and I immediately took us off the rolls. Mom and I never took another government handout.

It is hard for me to describe what I felt when I took this first job. The money I earned was mine; I was now the head of household and proud of it. Mom also recognized the change. No longer did she set curfews, and she relaxed other rules of the house to accommodate me. Soon I began asking my boss for additional work, like waxing the floors of the store on Sundays. Word got around to the other merchants in the area that I was a high school student who wanted to "make something of himself." Additional Sunday work came my way.

I was usually paid a flat $10 for a floor-waxing job that took about six hours to complete. On many Sundays, I waxed the floors at one store from six in the morning until noon, took a half-hour break for lunch, and then headed to another store, where I did more waxing from one to seven or eight at night. I was earning more on Sundays than I was getting for twenty-five hours each week at the Fabric Center. After about a year, I mustered up the nerve to ask my day-job bosses, Joe and Manny Schwartz, for a raise. They agreed that I was worth it and bumped me up to 75¢ an hour.

When Uncle James heard that I had taken this job, he came over to Mom's house to talk to me about it. He tried to make it a casual conversation, but as we talked about the details, I could tell he was pleased at the decision I had made, although he never said much more than "You doing good, Wardell, making your own way and earning your keep." His encouragement helped offset Mom's fears that my "false pride" in refusing welfare would lead to financial ruin and cost us everything. In time, of course, she forgot all about this and instead bragged to friends about how her "baby" had grown up so fast that he was now the man of the house. James helped me understand her position as a woman too old to work but too young for Social Security and thus in no position to understand the aspirations of a young venture capitalist.

I used the job at the Fabric Center as a stepping stone to a succession of other jobs as I worked my way through high school and college. I always kept James up to date about what I was doing—the hours I worked, the pay I made, the duties I had assumed. He was as interested in these facts as some men are in the box scores of baseball games. I once told James that one of my bosses had called me a "self-starter." It took him a moment to wrap his mind around this term. But when he did, his face bloomed into a wide grin. I don't think he would have been prouder if I had told him I had just received the Medal of Honor.

"You get yourself to church, boy!"

A Lesson about the Importance of Religion

When I was growing up, we attended Macedonia Baptist, a little church situated between the Sacramento communities of Del Paso Heights and Rio Linda. Church was the focus of our lives every Sunday, and the afterglow of the day's devotions suffused the remainder of the week.

The Sunday ritual was unalterable. Around eight o'clock in the morning, Brother Lester or Brother Dumas would swing by our house in the old rattletrap blue bus to pick up Mom and me for Sunday school. Aunt Bert and Uncle James would join us later for the eleven o'clock service that began a full day of worship. And it really took all day. If Pastor Cummings got fired up and the music tugged especially hard at our souls and all the sisters went rigid and had to be carried out by the brothers, the eleven o'clock service might last till two in the afternoon. Whenever it finished, the little blue bus would bring us home again, and Mom and Aunt Bert would cook a big meal, and James and I, along with sundry other relatives, would stuff ourselves. After that came a nap to sleep off the food and then it was time to get ready for the little blue bus when it returned at half past four to take us back to Macedonia Baptist for the five o'clock service.

Even when you dreaded it—*damn, got to spend all day in church,* I can hear myself muttering as I woke up Sunday morning—it was great, the one day of the week that was reliably filled with character and drama. In any case, I didn't have any choice about whether or not to participate. "You got to go to church, boy!" Uncle James insisted, enforcing the Fourth Commandment in his household. Every Sabbath, rain or shine, sick or well, he not only made sure that I answered the call, but put on his Sunday-go-to-meeting clothes like everyone else in the congregation and got ready for a day of God.

Mom was even more steadfast in devotion, immersing herself in the Word of God throughout the week and insisting that I do the same. She knew the Bible forward and backward. You could ask her what verse addressed such-and-such a problem, and she would cite it virtually word for word. She required that I read the Bible too. One of our rituals took place Saturday nights, when she would begin preparing the dough for the homemade rolls for Sunday's dinner and gave me assigned passages to read from the Good Book. (Even today I still think of the stern prophets of the Old Testament every time I smell the chemistry of yeast and flour.) The morality of the Bible was at times hard to live up to, but the language was always glorious and gave me the ambition of learning to write and talk the way that God and his chosen people did.

James was one of Macedonia Baptist's indispensable men. He served on the deacon board. He gave a sweat tithe by helping with the physical upkeep of the church. He was a pallbearer at funerals, where he would put an arm around the new widows and encourage them to cry on his shoulder. He was there at the baptismal font when new communicants got a full immersion in front of the entire congregation between Sunday school and the eleven o'clock service, and was often the one to announce, "Now you're washed in the blood of the Lamb." He vigilantly noted which assistant pastors were checking out the sweet-looking young women in the choir while Pastor Cummings was preaching, and stopped such flirtations with a steely gaze.

Sometimes Mom taught Sunday school; sometimes she sat with the children and monitored whoever happened to have replaced her as teacher on that particular day. When I turned thirteen, she encouraged me to teach a class of younger children. I often wasn't sure what I was doing, but I knew that I was following in Mom's and James' footsteps and this in itself made the experience meaningful. During the general service, I watched James for cues on how to react. With the music swelling the preacher's words into spectacle, I would sometimes catch his eye and join in an imperceptible shrug when Cousin Ora's "Amens" and hand fluttering became more pronounced as she prepared to pass out, having then to be carried outside—an event that happened most Sundays.

Uncle James was a spiritual man, and yet all this zealous participation at Macedonia Baptist notwithstanding, I'm not sure that he was deeply religious in any doctrinaire sense. For him, church was not just a place where the Word of God was spoken. It was also the place where we all renewed our ties to each other, ties that remained firmly knotted Monday through Saturday. James believed that church had a very positive effect, perhaps an invisible one but powerful nonetheless, out there on the streets, every day, influencing people to choose their good angels over their bad ones.

Was church morally necessary to have a good life? I think James felt that everyone had a basic knowledge of good and evil and shouldn't need someone else to tell them the difference. But he also appreciated the role of religion in helping propagate values that civilized the community. What was said at Macedonia Baptist and at countless other small congregations throughout Del Paso Heights helped keep the secular world sane. James was no sociologist, but he believed as firmly as Daniel Patrick Moynihan and other intellectuals that church was one of the few institutions that could help restrain the often-chaotic impulses of people on the streets.

James and the other elders wanted you at church not just to preach at you, but to teach you manners; to teach you how to act in public; to instill respect for old folks and an obligation to help the needy; to make you realize that the body was the temple of the spirit and so you shouldn't act in a destructive way with drugs and alcohol. They rendered unto Caesar by getting us young people to render unto God.

People like Sister Lester and Sister Dumas were not only watching you in church, but, because church extended into the community on weekdays, were watching you outside of church too. You had to be careful when you were out there rendering unto Caesar. It was not just these alpha church ladies who were enforcers. If any of the other church elders saw you misbehaving, they would not hesitate to call you out right there in the street and "signify" with a waving index finger and blunt reproaches. Then they would telephone or, even worse, visit your parents and report not just on what you had

Uncle James was most comfortable in his overalls, but on Sundays, he wore his "church clothes."

My Aunt Bert—Bertha Louis—was the love of James Louis's life.

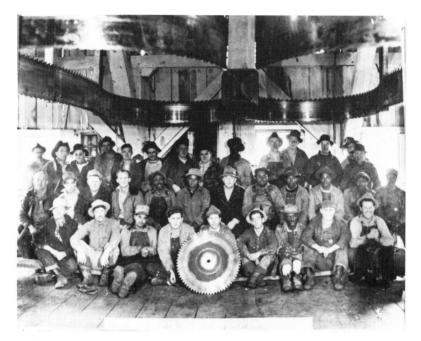

Uncle James and co-workers at the sawmill in Oregon House, California.

Piling lumber in the late 1940s, James Louis found dignity and meaning in his work.

Uncle James loved to hunt; his hounds were among his proudest possessions.

Uncle James, unfazed by racial stereotypes, relaxes with a slice of watermelon.

been observed saying or doing, but on how you had looked when saying or doing it.

James was downcast when Macedonia Baptist and the other churches in our community began to lose their influence to the value-free secularization that gained force after the 1960s. On the defensive, religion was unable any longer to play a central role in helping kids learn how to navigate a civilized society. James was especially appalled by the growing problem of single teenage mothers in the black community, and of thirty-year-old grandmothers living with fifteen-year-old mothers and their new babies in the same house, all three generations supported by the government, which had become the male of record in their lives. He associated this development with the proliferation of aimless young black men in baggy trousers with a butt crack showing, wearing hats with bills to the side, gangsta style, and always carrying a ghetto blaster or riding low in a car that had been transformed into a boom box. James knew something was terribly wrong because such young people were beyond the power of the church and the community it represented to mold them into respectable members of society. "These people need a good dose of God," he would sometimes say.

In James' later years, my cousin Phyllis and I often sat in the family room listening to him and Aunt Bert voice their disgust over the deteriorating moral character of young black people. James would finally get so frustrated that he would say someone needed to get a belt and use it to bring them back into line. When I explained to him that often no one was around in black households to do this, he would say, "That's the problem. Young girls are spreading their legs and having babies and the boys who do that to them just go off and get some other girl pregnant. They don't want to build families. They just want to pleasure themselves. And there's nothing left in our community to make them into better people."

On Sunday mornings these days I sometimes wake up with a vague feeling of anxiety. It always takes me a little while to identify the cause. Then I realize that some distant part of me is still waiting for that little blue bus to take us back to the church that played such a central role in our lives and helped supply the content of our community's character. The awareness that this bus has stopped running always brings a moment of melancholy.

"You don't feed that dog of yours, he's gonna starve."
A Lesson about Responsibility

James Louis loved dogs all his life. Most of those he owned over the years were junkyard dogs. He called them his "hounds," although most of them were actually mutts whose inner hound James had been liberating through his patient training techniques. He bred them himself, and they were a motley lot—mostly big dogs, some with outgoing personalities and others not the least bit interested in ingratiating themselves with humans in the manner of most pets. Some were outright scary. But they all loved James unconditionally and mistrusted everyone else. He took care of them the way he did his other possessions—keeping them in tiptop working order.

Not surprisingly, given James' approach to life, the dogs were not pampered pets but workers. Their first duty was to protect the house. This they did with enthusiasm, raising a yelping racket that made the back yard sound like the city pound whenever visitors came near—relatives or strangers. But the dogs' main job was hunting. This was Uncle James' passion. In good weather, he went out every weekend. In winter months when inclemency prevented him from working on the Teichert construction site, he piled his guns and his dogs into the pickup and headed for the hills. Hunting was sport, but it also put meat on the table. James and his dogs brought back deer, coons, possum, rabbit, even bear. James especially loved bear meat, although Aunt Bert considered it nasty stuff and cooked it only under protest.

When I was nine, James got me a dog of my own—a German shepherd. Like some of his, it was generically named "Shep." I immediately bonded with Shep and he became my best friend for a couple of years. But as I got older, my life pointed outward more, toward friends and away from family. As I spent more time away from home, I sometimes forgot about Shep. But James Louis wouldn't put up with it. While he was firm with animals, he wouldn't abide cruelty toward them. Most of all, he couldn't abide irresponsibility in caring for them. On occasion, if I had baseball practice or something else that I wanted to do after school, I thought it would be easy for him to take on the care of Shep since he was already caring for his own dogs. What difference did one more make?

But whenever I asked for this favor, James, who otherwise gave me pretty much whatever I asked for, not only refused but told me that my allowance and personal freedom would be conditioned on how well I took care of Shep. He repeatedly drove home the fact that if I didn't do the right thing, Shep would die because no one else was going to take care of the animal for me. I would come home one day and find him lying on the floor with his eyes closed and his tongue lolling out of the side of his mouth—killed by my irresponsibility. I tried to ignore Shep sometimes when I was with my friends. But I kept thinking of James' description of how he would appear in death, and this drew me home to look after him. As I learned to take care of Shep, I started taking care of other responsibilities too.

Later on, I realized that for James, responsibility wasn't an onerous duty to be sullenly discharged with clenched teeth and a closed heart. It was a privilege to be responsible for something or someone other than yourself. It meant that you were connected and intrinsically dependable. James was a provider for his family (and the dogs were part of this family), and he welcomed the fact that we all counted on him. Aunt Bert and I never worried about whether there would be food on the table, clothes on our backs, or a roof over our head. And this was because James had made it his life's work to be dependable. He liked taking things on his own broad shoulders. It was part of being a *mane.* If I have come to feel this way too—and I've spent a lifetime trying to make it so—the lesson began with Shep.

Even today, when I'm tempted to let my responsibilities slack, I always feel James Louis looking over my shoulder and asking if I want that dog of mine to starve to death because I didn't do the right thing.

It was this lesson that has convinced me that all children should be encouraged to be responsible for caring for a pet—a goldfish, bird, cat or dog—as a way of instilling a sense of responsibility in them.

"If you don't have mother wit, nothing else you have is going to help."

A Lesson about Common Sense

Uncle James had a great ability to size people up. He could speak with a person for a few minutes and tell what he was all about. This ability, he believed, came from his "mother wit." When he wanted to aim a killing insult at someone, he would allow a look of disgust to cross his face and say, "That man don't have no mother wit." James had a lot of respect for book learning; but it wasn't a substitute for mother wit—a quality he believed you were born with but might misplace or even lose on your way through life. If that happened, it was bad news for you.

James wanted to make sure that my mother wit was fully engaged. When I was a teenager, for instance, he often made a point of giving me a task but not telling me how to complete it. "You just go on and fool around with it," he'd reply when I demanded instructions. "You'll understand the common sense of it." Invariably I would complain. James would reply, "No, if I have to tell you how to do something, I may as well do it myself. Figure it out yourself and you'll never forget."

At the time, I was frustrated by the whole idea of trial and error. But eventually I came to appreciate the value of working my way through the maze of a complex task. James always judged me by the results and not the method used to achieve them. He never insisted that I do it his way. He just insisted that I do it well. Sometimes he admitted with pleasurable surprise that the solutions he had essentially forced me to discover were better than those he had assumed were correct.

"Mother wit" was about practical solutions to practical problems. But there was a more profound dimension to it as well. Exercising your mother wit allowed you to see things clearly and honestly in a way that did justice to an event or occasion; it helped you avoid the moral laziness of easy explanations and the pompousness of over-intellectualized ones.

Mother wit was also the still, small voice inside that kept you grounded, as I saw one afternoon following the campaign for Proposition 209. I had traveled to San Francisco for the California Building Industry Association's annual Hall of Fame dinner, and after checking in at the St. Francis Hotel and starting up to my room, I realized that I had left my briefcase in the car. Heading back to the hotel parking garage, I got off the elevator at the basement and immediately bumped into a couple of elderly white men who were looking around in a somewhat disoriented way. One of them said, "Excuse me, are you the man who unlocks the meeting room?"

I did an intellectual double take and then, my racial hackles rising, answered with as much irritation as I could pack into my voice: "No, I'm *not* the man who unlocks the rooms."

The two white men shrank back and I walked on, fuming to myself about how racial profiling is practiced every day in subtle forms by people who would otherwise piously condemn it in state troopers working the New Jersey Turnpike. But my anger didn't feel very good after the first rush of self-righteousness. I stopped and forced myself to take stock of the situation. Yes, the men I had just encountered had seen someone who was "black," someone who was also without luggage, striding purposefully out of the elevator as if on a task, and dressed in a semi-uniform of blazer and gray slacks.

I turned around and retraced my steps.

"What made you think I was the guy who unlocks the meeting rooms?" I asked the two men when I caught up with them.

"Well, you were dressed a little like a hotel employee, sir," the one who had spoken earlier answered in a deferential way. "Believe me, I meant no insult."

"Well, I hope you'll forgive me for being abrupt," I said. I shook their hands and headed back toward my car, relieved that the burden of racial self-pity had been lifted off my shoulders. I imagined James Louis chuckling over the fact that mother wit had saved me from a bout of foolishness.

"Go get yourself educated. They can't take that away from you."

A Lesson about Learning

J ames Louis didn't make it past the third grade. He was shrewd enough about life and confident enough in his judgments that this deficit didn't bother him, except when it came to reading and writing. Signing his name was not only a chore, but a task that caused him a metaphysical lurch whenever he had to take it on.

Every Friday afternoon he would come home after work and hand his check to Aunt Bert. She would stare at it for a moment and then hand it back and go get a pen. When she asked him to endorse the check for her to deposit at the bank, a look of incredible sadness would flit over his face, soon replaced by a look of exasperation.

"Bert, get me a beer, will you?" he'd say, sitting down at the kitchen table with an air of resignation. Aunt Bert would bring him a beer and he would begin to sip it slowly, summoning his confidence. Then he would hold the check up to the light as if to inspect it for forgery. Finally, having finished the beer and run out of procrastinations, he would end the weekly ritual by grasping the pen that Aunt Bert handed him and inscribing a few small circles in the air to warm up before laboriously writing his name on the check. It seemed to take a very long time. I always noticed that the individual letters were never completely joined up in his version of cursive.

By comparison, I was his own homegrown prodigy, doing well in the schools that I attended, first in Bremerton and then in Sacramento. Uncle James was fiercely proud of me. "You go on and get yourself an education," he said to me more than once when I complained about homework. "They can't take that away from you." At the time, I didn't know who "they" were or why they would consider stealing a little learning, but later on I understood that James felt that his own right to an education had been stolen from him by a racist regime that had left him a man for whom writing was a chore. Yet he never complained about his lot in life; he simply made the best of the cards that had been dealt to him.

As I reached the end of my senior year at Grant Union High School, James kept asking me about college. I told him that I was going, but didn't know where. If some counselor had come to Grant and helped me apply for a scholarship for needy students, I might have wound up at Berkeley or UCLA, campuses that my grades and aptitude tests qualified me to attend. But there weren't any such counselors or scholarships in 1957. (In many inner-city schools there still aren't; and the strident defenders of affirmative action rarely show up there to help poor students who might qualify for elite campuses if they had person-to-person assistance during the application process.) I ended up going to American River Junior College because there were three other graduating Grant seniors from my neighborhood who planned to go there, and not having a car, I went where the carpool went.

As the first person in my family to get through high school, let alone attend college, I felt that I was in terra incognito during my first couple of semesters at ARJC. As I worried about how to fit in, I always felt James' gaze on me—not critical, but quizzical, interested in how I would handle this challenge and checking to make sure I wasn't going to use my education to pretend that I was better than others. To him, this would have been "putting on airs"—definitely a bad thing.

During my years as a Regent of the University of California, I was struck by just how segregated higher education was—"voluntarily" segregated, perhaps, but segregated nonetheless. At many of the UC campuses there were segregated dorms, segregated graduations, and even a segregated curriculum in which black students are disproportionately lured into majoring in ethnic studies, the weakest and most intellectually compromised offerings at the university.

In the late 1950s and early 1960s, when racial prejudice was far more prevalent than it is today, I experienced none of this separatism. After two years in junior college, I had saved enough money from my jobs to transfer to a four-year school, Sacramento State College. My first week on campus, I decided to join a fraternity, eventually choosing Delta Phi Omega. DPO had never had a black member, but I didn't know this until after I had made my commitment and my sponsor casually said one day that we were going to break a racial barrier. This was the first and only time during the nearly three years I lived in the DPO house that my color was ever mentioned.

The members of Delta Phi Omega ate and studied together, lived together, and were constant companions at social events. We were all very different, but we were "brothers" by choice, not by some accident of color. Looking back, I believe that there was far more real "diversity" in that fraternity house than in the racially orthodox residences of most college campuses today.

At the end of my junior year, I was elected student body president of "Sac State." As the first black to hold this position, I was sometimes referred to as a "trailblazer," although I didn't think of myself in such terms. (To be honest, one of the reasons I wanted the job was that it paid $35 a month and carried parking privileges along with it.) Uncle James, who had broken into one of his wide grins when he heard of my election, supported me in declining to play the racial pioneer. "You don't have to see your color all the time," he told me. "If others do, that's their problem. Best thing is to just get along with life."

⚊◆⚊

I went through college with a sort of sadness, fearing that the experience would alienate me from James and the rest of my family. I had seen this happen to other students with backgrounds similar to mine: their growing sophistication set down fault lines between them and their less-educated parents. In this regard, I was prepared for the worst and resigned myself to the cost of the new vistas opening up to me—that they would make James appear smaller and more ignorant than the larger-than-life figure who had sheltered and taught me in my growing up. In fact, however, what I experienced did much more to confirm than to diminish Uncle James.

In my first semester at Sac State, I was lucky enough to take a course called Elements of Western Political Theory from Dr. Robert Thompson, a tall and gangly man with a bearded face and a laconic manner. He had a way of asking questions—tilting his head forward and peering down over half glasses—in a Socratic process that brought out the best in his students. He was one of those natural-born teachers who instruct not only by what they say, but even more by who they are. (And in this, it occurred to me later on, he was similar to James Louis himself.)

The year after I took his course, Dr. Thompson hired me as his reader to help grade student papers. We spent a lot of time talking about the problems and promise inherent in the American Dream, a popular subject in 1960. Sitting in his cramped office one day after a lecture, I challenged his premise that I had been created equal to some other students who were born with silver spoons in their mouths. During my summer vacation, after all, I had worked from eight at night until three in the morning on the assembly line at Continental Can Company and then went back to the fraternity house to catch a few hours of sleep before working a half day as a recreation supervisor at a local children's home. Most of the other students didn't have to work at all; they had nice cars and ample allowances, and had entered life well ahead of me.

"Mr. Connerly," Dr. Thompson replied (in all the years I knew him he never called me by my first name), "life is imperfect, and the *ideal* of all men being created equal is as important as the reality. What we want is for our government to *believe* that you and I are equal and to treat us accordingly in its transactions. Then, in the most basic sense, we are, indeed, created equal." When he said this, I remember thinking to myself that I had already heard something like this, although in rougher-hewn terms, from my Uncle James.

Dr. Thompson was a realist. He pointed out—and this was in the full flush of optimism of the early civil rights movement—that equal opportunity, when it finally came, wouldn't necessarily lead to equal outcomes, and that this was sure to cause problems. But he was also an idealist and believed that the egalitarian spirit in America would ultimately allow all people to move upward in the social and economic order based on their individual talents and efforts. He was right, and it is a shame that this perspective is so out of fashion in the academy today.

The only time in our long acquaintance when Dr. Thompson mentioned my own race was at dinner at his house one evening in the fall of 1961. We had been talking about the revolution that Martin Luther King Jr. was generating in the South. Dr. Thompson said if it succeeded in its aims, it would redeem America. Then he looked at me over his glasses and said, "Mr. Connerly, when the day comes that I can call you a son of a bitch without you thinking that I am a bigot, or thinking about my color in relation to yours, that will be the day when true equality will have been achieved."

A defining moment during my tenure as student body president at Sac State came when an Asian student was hit by a truck and killed while riding his motorbike to campus. I knew that this man (who had a wife and several children back home and was looking to bring them to this country when he completed his engineering degree) had tried to rent an apartment in River Park, a neighborhood within walking distance of the campus, but had been turned down because he was a dark-skinned foreigner. He was forced to take a place several miles away and had to make a long trip on his motorbike every morning in dangerous traffic.

I convinced the student council to take this matter up and create a Committee against Discrimination in Housing. When the committee was formed, I was selected to be its chairman. Our investigation showed that many other minority students had also experienced discrimination. When word leaked out about the committee's findings, I was contacted by the office of Jesse Unruh, at that time the "Big Daddy" of Democratic Party politics in California and Speaker of the California Assembly, and asked to testify before the legislature. I did so and publicly announced that race discrimination existed "right here in River City."

Soon after, I got an invitation from Dr. Guy West, Sac State's president, for dinner at his official quarters. It was a genteel occasion, but the agenda was not very well hidden: to get me to drop the appearance before the legislature and let the whole issue of local housing discrimination and its effect on Sac State students disappear—through benign neglect, so to speak. There were no threats, of course, but I came away with the feeling that my future would be much better, at Sac State and after graduation, if I kept my mouth shut.

The next day I went to Dr. Thompson and told him what had happened.

"What should I do?" I asked after finishing the story.

"You've got to consult your 'knower,'" Thompson smiled.

"What's that?"

"Your heart, your conscience, your gut, your *knower*," he shrugged. "What does your knower tell you to do?"

"That I don't want to back down," I replied.

"Well," he chuckled, "listen to your knower."

As I left his office, I realized that Dr. Thompson's "knower" was a kissing cousin to James Louis's "mother wit"—the needle on the moral compass that steers you in the right direction. I testified before the legislature. Afterward, our Committee against Discrimination in Housing released a report that gave a push to the passage of the Rumsford Fair Housing Act, which ultimately outlawed throughout California the kind of housing discrimination we had documented in Sacramento.

I felt that I had been educated, and that the insights I had acquired would never be taken away from me.

"Don't judge a book by its cover."
A Lesson about People

James Louis saw every person he met as an individual. This trait did not come from some kind of politically correct dogma; it came from his inborn inclination to treat others with respect. Whatever their position in life, people were just people to Uncle James. I am sure he would have shot a withering look at someone who urged him to "celebrate diversity." But he definitely believed in the Golden Rule.

My cousin Phyllis often says of her father that he never met a stranger. I think she's right: Uncle James had a genius for friendship, and it came from two sources. First, he never talked much about himself. He was a natural listener, as adept at drawing people out through his unfeigned interest in what they were saying as any journalist I've ever met. As a consequence, the people he met, glad that someone cared enough to listen, opened up to him and soon forgot that they were doing all the talking.

The second and more important quality that allowed James to relate so well to people was his belief that the surface differences that distinguish us from each other are far less important than our common humanity—a cliché only to those who pay lip service to this idea without really believing in it.

Occasionally I would accompany James and his hounds on one of their weekend hunting expeditions. It was not infrequent for one of the dogs to stray off and be unable to locate the scent leading back to the pickup before it was time for us to leave for home. After waiting and searching until long past dark, Uncle James would go to the nearby houses, knock on the doors, and tell the occupants that he was a hunter and had lost one of his hounds. He would then describe the dog, tell them its name, and leave his telephone number with a request that they call him if they saw an animal fitting its description.

Almost always, Aunt Bert would get a call by the middle of the week from someone who wanted to let her know that the dog had been found and would be kept until James showed up to claim it. And so, as soon as he got off work on Friday, the two of us would get in the pickup and drive to the property of the caller to retrieve the hound.

This transaction usually involved more than the return of an animal. At James' subtle urging, the person who had tended the dog for him would launch into a detailed explanation about how the animal had been found and how it had behaved since then. This would lead to a meandering conversation about hunting, hounds, land use rights, forestry management, and other such things. As the two parties discovered that they had much in common, the man who had called (it was always a man and usually a fellow dog lover) would invite James and me to come into the house for a while. After more genial talk, we would be invited to stay for

lunch. Although Aunt Bert had packed enough sandwiches and soft drinks to last us a month, Uncle James
always accepted the offer. Once, when we were on the
way home after one of these occasions, I asked him why
he had accepted the dinner invitation knowing that Aunt
Bert had provided us with such an abundance of food of
our own. He gave me a look as if I were dim: "These people go out and look for our hound, feed and keep him till
we git here, and then they offer to make supper for us,
and we ain't gonna eat? What's the matter with you?"

Many black people would have been wary of some of
the individuals with whom we had broken bread because
they were country "rednecks." (Most did fit the stereo-
type: large, bearded men in overalls, whose front yards
were cluttered with the rusting hulks of derelict auto-
mobiles.) And it was probably true that some of these
rednecks began by seeing James Louis as just another
"colored man." But he won them over—without really
trying to—by his love of animals and of conversation, and
by the fact that he didn't make any assumptions about
them because of how they looked or lived. As a result,
potential barriers—of race or class or income or outlook—never came into play, and sometimes what began
as casual contacts became lasting relationships.

Years after James had regretfully been forced by the
debilitations of old age to give up hunting, I still traveled
up into the foothills where he and his dogs had ranged
for many years. My daughter was then in the high school
band and I had joined with other parents to form a band
boosters club. One of our projects was to help our kids
raise money for their band activities by buying Christmas trees and wreaths and then reselling them in Sacramento during the holiday season.

One of our suppliers—Larry was his name—had hundreds of acres of fir and pine about fifty miles up in the foothills. Long after my daughter had graduated, I would still drive to his ranch each year to purchase dozens of wreaths and give them to clients and friends as holiday gifts. Even after nearly a decade of doing business, there was only the most tenuous of bonds between Larry, the rural seller of Christmas trees and wreaths, and me, the city slicker who bought them. I liked him but didn't really know him, and I think the feeling was mutual.

One year, I invited Uncle James to join me on this annual trek. He readily accepted. The drive reminded me of those earlier times when we went to retrieve one of his hounds, only now I was the driver and the mission was mine. Or so I thought. When we arrived at Larry's property and I introduced him to Uncle James, they took to each other immediately. As we stood by the campfire drinking coffee outside the tree farm's office trailer, they began to share stories about hunting and living in the country. Larry invited us to stay for lunch with him— something that had never happened in the decade that I had been doing business with him. By the time we left, he was clapping James familiarly on the shoulder.

Every year thereafter, the first thing Larry would say upon my arrival at his property was, "How's James? Why didn't you bring him?" On that one visit they had agreed that Uncle James would return to go hunting, and Larry was looking forward to it. Uncle James' worsening health and eventual death prevented him from fulfilling that commitment.

The uncanny ability that James Louis had to relate to "strangers" in such a way that immediate connections were made was something I always envied. I could never figure out exactly the formula that created this instant chemistry with people he had never previously met. I think it had to do with the fact that he never feared that the other parties might be using these transactions for some kind of secret advantage, because he himself was incapable of such a thing.

For many years, I have waged a very high-profile campaign to make America move closer to the perfect union to which it aspires by abandoning preferences based on race, color, sex, ethnicity and national origin. In the course of this campaign, I have learned a few things about people. But nothing compares to the basic lesson I learned from Uncle James about treating everyone you encounter with decency and respect. This is partly a variation of the injunction to "do unto others." It is also a reminder not to allow yourself to think you're a "big shot," a term that James always uttered with contempt.

⊨◆⊨

There is one other thing about Uncle James' way of relating to people that is more consequential than it may seem. He always addressed every new person he met and every elderly person as "sir" or "ma'am." In part, it was a habit left over from his Southern upbringing; it was also his own instinctive way of showing courtesy. Somewhere in his life, this simple and uneducated man had seen something that eludes most of us: that addressing others with words of formal respect helps remove the psychological obstructions that separate people from each other.

Following James—and with a nod to my own briefly experienced Southern heritage—I too began my life by referring to others as "sir" or "ma'am." But I got out of this habit over the years, partly because of the informality of California manners and partly because, beginning in the 1960s, such respectfulness from a young black man had taken on the stigma of being overly deferential. But I was reminded not long ago of how important this very simple practice can be in "civilizing" possibly abrasive discussions.

In the spring of 2007, I was the guest lecturer at a community forum sponsored by Philander Smith College, a "historically black college" in Little Rock, Arkansas. I had made many other such appearances after becoming identified with the movement against race preferences. In many of these campus appearances, protestors drowned me out before I could get out a single sentence. I was always less bothered by the hostility of the radical students who had contempt for my free speech, than by my sadness that the kids in the audience who wanted to support my position were also intimidated into silence. And I was bothered too by the fact that in almost all of these instances, the college administrators present for my speech stood by impassively and let the chaos happen. To them, the university was not a free marketplace of ideas, but an echo chamber for politically correct ideas. These administrators, who allowed me to be silenced and at times physically threatened, would have been outraged if the same thing had happened to Angela Davis, longtime supporter of Stalinist causes, or to professional anti-Americans such as Ward Churchill and Cindy Sheehan.

I have to admit that I braced myself (as usual) when I got up to speak at Philander Smith. But this event turned out to be one of the most respectful and productive exchanges in which I have participated during all the years of my involvement in the public debate about race. What made it so was the mutual respect that the president of the college, Dr. James Kimborough, the faculty and staff, the students, and most of those from the Little Rock community exhibited. Virtually every question to me from the audience began with "sir." I found myself replying in kind.

It is very difficult to hurl invectives at someone whom you have just addressed with such civility. And, indeed, I felt that the event at Philander Smith involved a real dialogue. Not everyone in the audience agreed with me that race preferences are the flip side of the coin of racial discrimination. But many did, and others who heard my talk and the discussion that followed had obviously come around to this position by the time the event ended. For my part, I understood some of the doubts raised in a way that was impossible when done in an atmosphere inflamed by hatred and aggression.

I was not the only beneficiary of respect from the Philander community. The debate itself benefited as well. I left Little Rock the next day feeling that I had just experienced something Uncle James would have understood very well. As I listened to the political debates during the 2008 presidential campaign season, I found myself amused whenever Senator John McCain would address his audience as "my friends." Although such a practice can become a tad tiring, I am reminded of my experience at Philander Smith and how such respectful references can pave the way for a more civil discussion. So . . . my friends!

"The smallest pancake has two sides."

A Lesson about Perspective

Whenever he thought I was getting a bit "uppity"—a word he sometimes used to describe someone who pursued his ideas too aggressively—James would give me a sly look out of the corner of his eye and remind me that "the smallest pancake has two sides," miming as he said this the motion of someone using a spatula to pry up a concept in order to check out what might be underneath.

He employed this phrase often during my college years and right after, a time when I was coming into the world of ideas and was learning, in the way of newly educated young people, to make my case by heedlessly steamrolling other possible positions. At the time, James' admonition sometimes annoyed me: I wanted to follow what seemed the implacable logic of my argumentation without having to worry about someone reminding me to see the other side. But I could never quite ignore that image of the pancake on the griddle, waiting to be flipped over and reveal a whole new side.

This image has stayed with me, even in my unexpected second career as spokesman for colorblindness and against race preferences, when I have felt more committed—and, to be honest, more right—about what I am doing than at any other point in my life. Since getting into this struggle, I have never had any doubt that the metastasizing system of race preferences of the 1990s was morally rancid and socially destructive, creating a vast regime of politically correct discrimination filled with the same bureaucratic rules and obsession with blood quantum that characterized Jim Crow. The argument over this issue has been intense for the last thirteen years, and I have pressed my case as strenuously as I could, from 1995, when as chairman of the Finance Committee of the Board of Regents I first helped eliminate preferences from the University of California's student selection process, until today, when I am trying to pass initiatives in states all over the country modeled on the epochal 1964 Civil Rights Act. But at the same time that I've tried to argue my case as strenuously as I can, I have also always been aware that this particular pancake has another side. And this awareness, interestingly enough, has made me an even more passionate advocate against race preferences than I would otherwise have been.

When I first got involved in this issue at the University of California over fourteen years ago, I thought that it was never justifiable, in any circumstances, to use skin color as a criterion for granting advantages in the public square. But as I listened to the fierce commitment of my more honorable opponents in this debate—those who were not arguing from a knee-jerk anti-American perspective in which our country is, if anything, more racist today than it was during the era of slavery—and began to look back at the history of affirmative action and think of the huge strides our country had made when state-sanctioned discrimination was finally vanquished in the 1960s, I saw that things would not have turned around so quickly for blacks and with relatively little social turbulence had there not been some degree of color-consciousness.

In 1961, JFK issued Executive Order 10925 to mandate aggressive nondiscrimination. In announcing that order, President Kennedy said that "Race has no place in American life and law." I live by this creed. After his assassination, the 1964 Civil Rights Act, which enshrines nondiscrimination as the nation's basic philosophy, was passed as a tribute to Kennedy. But some civil rights advocates said that legal equality was not enough for a group such as American blacks, who had been so systematically discriminated against and historically disadvantaged. Lyndon Johnson agreed with them. As he said at the time, you don't take the chains off a man and immediately bring him to the starting line of a race and expect that he will be able to compete equally.

I have never wavered in my belief that it is always a mistake to force government agencies to look at race and put a discriminatory thumb on the social scale. Yet I have also understood that race-consciousness in the crucial period of the 1960s may have kept us from far more damaging social upheaval than we actually experienced. The affirmative remedy should have been limited to blacks, with sunset provisions built in to prevent the sort of "mission creep" that soon appeared. These conditions should have been enacted by Congress, so that the courts would not have been forced to define haphazardly the direction that affirmative action has taken over the past four-plus decades.

But this wasn't done. Instead, Pandora's box was opened and out sprang a preference regime that made equal-opportunity victims out of women and an ever-expanding universe of minority groups, most of which had nothing even remotely comparable to the historical experience of blacks in American life. Rather than a brief and targeted remedy, preferences and the self-justifying bureaucracy that enforced them took hold as a flawed social policy. (Even Justice Sandra Day O'Connor, author of a deeply incoherent Supreme Court decision extending the lifespan of affirmative action, noted in passing that it was hard to enshrine something that the Constitution barely tolerates.)

As I have considered the case of my opponents and tried to understand how their initial idealism about bringing us all to the starting line together developed into a Frankenstein monster, it has occurred to me that perhaps we had to see what a comprehensive system of preferences would look like in order to demystify the allure that affirmative action might otherwise have had as an ideal road not taken.

"I'm here with you, ain't I?"
A Lesson about Love

Although James Louis might talk with pleasure to a perfect stranger about a variety of subjects, ranging from the weather to politics, he held intimate matters close to his vest. We never knew when he was sick, for instance, because he wouldn't tell us. This sense of privacy was even more the case when it came to feelings and emotions. He was not the sort of person to wear his heart on his sleeve. His view was that a man's feelings are his alone and he should not inflict them on others.

But while he never told us what he felt for us, we always knew because of the way he acted toward us. And as he always reminded us, "actions speak louder than words."

James showed his love in his cheerfulness. He was no Pollyanna; indeed, he had a strong sense of life's cruel vagaries. But he wouldn't countenance those who complained about their fate. He buoyed the rest of us by looking on the bright side, cracking jokes, extracting humor out of everyday events.

Television today, for instance, is considered by many parents to be an enemy; but in our family it was a chance to be together and have a common experience. James made sure that it was an interactive occasion. On Friday nights, when Gillette presented boxing matches, he insisted that we all watch. He liked the athletic welter and middle weights—Sugar Ray most of all, but also great club fighters like Kid Gavilan, Gene Fullmer and Carmen Basillio—and between rounds he would sometimes bob and weave and shoot out jabs followed by right crosses as if he too were in the fight. As the boxers answered the bell, he sat back in his chair and began a running commentary that was so colorful and true that we could shut down the sound on the television set. If there was any punch below the belt or action that seemed unfair, he would yell his displeasure. And once a contestant was in trouble, James always wanted the fight to be stopped.

On Tuesday it was *Sanford and Son,* our favorite program. James would warm up the small crowd in our living room by shuffling toward his seat in the distinctive gait that Red Foxx had given his character and say, "Well, look here who's coming." He had us in stitches long before we heard Foxx's gravelly voice.

James and Aunt Bert had as deep a bond as any I ever saw between two people. They were more like mates than married people. I never saw a saccharine emotion or a moment of false sentiment between them, and this was primarily because of James Louis. He expressed his emotions forcefully but without sentimentality, using irony to keep things in perspective. He always told Aunt Bert how much he cared for her, for instance, through a sort of comedy routine. It began with her chiding him for not buying her flowers for some special occasion. James would chuckle and say, "Why do I need to buy you flowers? I've planted a whole yard of 'em for ya, haven't I?" She would allow that this was so and then chivvy him further by saying, "James, you never tell me you love me." He'd get a sly look on his face and say, "I'm here witcha, ain't I?" Later on, while watching some television show, Bert would see a good-looking girl and say, "I'll bet you'd like someone like that, wouldn't you, James?" He'd look at her with pure adoration and say, "Hell, yeah, I would."

She'd give him back as good as she got, sometimes sweetly asking, "What do you want for lunch today, James?" He'd consider for a moment and reply, "Fix me up a sammitch from that roast left over from the other night, will you?" Then she'd flounce out of the dining room saying, "If you want a sandwich, you fix it yourself. You got two feet." And James would collapse in laughter.

Uncle James would never retire for the evening unless his car had at least three-quarters of a tank full of gas. When Aunt Bert would make fun of him for such idiosyncrasies, he would give her a sly smile and say, "What if one of you gets sick in the middle of the night? You won't make fun when I need to drive yo' ass to the hospital, will ya?"

When I read Shakespeare in college, I realized that Bert and James were like a black version of Beatrice and Benedict. Their verbal duels were their means of expressing a deep and abiding love without becoming smarmy. The words were a way of showing that they were living in the middle of their relationship and paying attention to its needs. From James' point of view, however, his responses to Bert were also a reminder that words were cheap and that everyone—himself included—should be judged on what they did rather than what they said. It was the perception of someone who didn't have easy access to words himself; who had watched and listened carefully to people who did, and saw that language was often a substitute for sincerity rather than an expression of it.

We live in a different time from the one in which James Louis lived. In his era it was unacceptable for a *mane* to compulsively remind those close to him how much he loved them. But he put food on the table and a roof over my head; he taught me how to look after myself; he helped get me through school and on the road to success. I sometimes wonder if the same thing can be said of today's sensitive males who often and easily express their love but then use it as the squid's ink to disappear when called to demonstrate real commitment.

"You don't bite the hand that feeds you."

A Lesson about Country

One of James Louis's favorite songs was the one by Merle Haggard with the lyrics about those who don't love this country being "on the wrong side of me." When he heard someone criticizing America in what seemed to him an unjust or disrespectful way, Uncle James always called the offender to account, saying, "You don't bite the hand that feeds you." He believed that this country, while not without flaws, had nonetheless given us the opportunity to lead a good life and that we owed it our strong allegiance. He had no patience with people who ran America down, and he became incensed when the antiwar protests and Black Power demonstrations of the late 1960s turned what had begun as constructive movements for social change in the direction of nihilism and a bitter hatred of the United States.

Having come of age in the segregated South, where he had suffered for his proudly independent streak, James knew as well as anyone how profoundly untrue to itself the country had been in the matter of race. But he also knew how unique the United States was among nations in its ability to look into its own heart, admit its errors, and change its course. Among the things I vividly recall from that 1950 trip into the heart of the Mississippi darkness was how James had spent our days there in Natchez looking around quizzically like some ethnographer trying to understand the folkways of a foreign country. *This is not America,* the look on his face said; *this is another country.* When we started back home, his spirit picked up; and when we passed over the state line that delivered us to California, he stopped the car, got out, and literally kissed the ground beside the highway.

In discussions with friends, James would always insist, "This here the best country." In using this phrase, he was taking a stand alongside those who affirmed with a clear eye America's uniqueness and exceptionalism. In a time when patriotism had become unfashionable because of Vietnam, especially among young blacks, he was not reluctant to profess his love of country publicly—standing defiantly at attention when the flag was raised at some sporting event and reverently putting his burly hand over his heart when the national anthem was sung or played, even at home while he was watching television.

While others were glorifying them as ghetto rebels, James saw the Black Panthers—and other groups that crossed over the line separating politics from criminality—for the con men and gangsters they were. He felt the same way about Stokely Carmichael and all the other "professional blacks" who emerged from the 1960s spewing their anti-American hatred.

I recall sitting with Aunt Bert, Uncle James and Phyllis on one occasion to watch the Summer Olympics. One of the black sprinters competing for America had won his race and was standing on the platform to receive his gold medal. As "The Star-Spangled Banner" was being played, the young man gazed off into the distance, expressing indirectly his obvious contempt for the patriotic moment. Watching this, Uncle James became irate and yelled at the screen, "Put your damn hand on your heart, boy, and show some respect." I shudder to think of how he would react to the sermon of Senator Barack Obama's pastor, Jeremiah Wright, who urged his congregation to profess that "God damn America" instead of "God bless America."

Martin Luther King Jr. was James Louis's hero. Uncle James watched the progress of the civil rights campaign in the South during the 1950s and 1960s in the same way that people during World War II had tracked the Allied advance in Europe and the Pacific on maps. Like most Americans and especially black people, he followed what was taking place in Alabama and Mississippi on the radio, always his favorite news medium. (In his old age, he was an enthusiastic listener of the program that Rush Limbaugh had on local Sacramento radio before becoming a national personality.) James never doubted that black people would overcome, and he believed that when they did, it would be not only because of their own brave efforts but because most of their white countrymen would be behind them.

I think that James was dizzied by the changes in how race was viewed during his lifetime. Starting out as "colored," he had become a Negro, then a black man, then an African American (although he hated this construction), and finally, completing the loop, a "person of color," the term of art for the multiculturalists. When we discussed all these linguistic contortions, he would finally shake his head and chuckle dubiously, and I knew what he was thinking: *A mane ain't nothing but a mane.*

James Louis felt no sympathy for the genealogy craze that swept the black community in the 1970s as a result of *Roots,* and he had no interest in discovering his own ancestral Kunta Kinte. Nor did he have any patience with what Teddy Roosevelt once called "hyphenated Americanism." When "African American" came into vogue in the 1980s, Uncle James made it clear that he felt this term had nothing to do with him. While he was vaguely amused by the sudden appearance of dashikis in the black community, he considered Afrocentrism the equivalent of witchcraft. "I'm a black man and that's all there is to it," James would say when the subject came up. "I don't know a damn thing about Africa and I don't want to know. All I know about Africa is that it's where we would still be if our ancestors didn't get lucky back all those years ago and get brought to America."

James didn't pay much attention to the politically correct racial classifications that replaced those he had grown up with. When push came to shove, people were pretty much what they had always been to him: "Mexican," not "Hispanic" or "Latino"; "Chinese" (even if they might be Japanese), not "Asian"; "Indian," not "Native American"; and so on. But it really didn't matter to James what they were called. He was actually one of the few people I've ever known who actually dealt with people on the basis of their character rather than their color. James would have laughed at the rich absurdity of the politically correct formulations ("to get beyond racism, we must first take race into account," etc.) that litter our social dialogue today.

For James Louis, the Promised Land was here and now—being able to conduct his life without interference; relying on government to discharge its responsibilities but not feeling governed during his waking hours; knowing that he was a stakeholder in the most generous and humane country in the world.

James Louis (1916–1996)

In 1936, at the height of the Depression, the writer James Agee toured the South for *Fortune* magazine and reported on conditions among sharecropper families there. What he saw became the basis for his great book *Let Us Now Praise Famous Men.* This work was a tribute to the resilience and bravery of these otherwise anonymous people whose grace and endurance shone through the social tragedy that had overtaken them.

I've always thought of James Louis as such a "famous man"—not well known outside his immediate family, working hard to scratch out a living, filled with hope and optimism even when the future seemed dim, a man in full despite the social disadvantages that constituted his birthright. I think of Uncle James whenever I see a black man shining shoes or checking luggage at the airport. These individuals are a reminder of the "famous men" who would honorably do whatever was necessary to be productive in our nation, certain that the day would come when their children would no longer be required to fill such roles in our society. It was their character that has made it possible for the likes of Senator Barack Obama to become a serious candidate for president of the United States, and for me to nudge my country in the direction of living out the "true meaning of our creed"—to respect the individuality of every American and to treat ourselves as individuals rather than "representatives" of some group or "race."

It may seem odd to speak of the "vision" of someone who didn't get past the third grade and was practically illiterate. Yet James' life was filled with that combination of zest and seriousness, tenderness and strength that marks the best of men. He had a coherent and compelling sense of individuality, citizenship and humanity, and of how important it was to honorably discharge the duties inherent in each of these categories. His actions and outlook were a sort of curriculum for the moral life. He would never have thought of himself as a teacher, but the way he comported himself was educational for those of us who were close to him. The language in which he taught was simple; but the life lessons themselves were profound.

His was a folk wisdom formulated in the simple, almost ritual terms of a bygone era. We have moved on to self-help experts, relationship consultants, human potential gurus—each with their own technical vocabulary. I would put James Louis up against any of them with confidence that his approach to life would be more likely to create a happy and productive individual than any of theirs.

I remember once when James pointed out to me an obituary of an acquaintance in the *Sacramento Bee.* He put his stubby forefinger on the dash between the dead person's birth and death dates and said, "Where you start and where you end don't matter. It's how you fill up that space right there that counts."

The space between his own beginning and ending was not only full, but brimming over; and I am eternally grateful for the lessons he taught me. As we observe the political landscape of our nation, we find sex scandals, a frequent unwillingness to be forthright in defense of one's beliefs, and the desire to defeat one's opponents at all costs. As we view the growing crassness of our culture, we find laziness, disrespect for human life, vulgarity, and an "anything goes" attitude that is brought to the public arena. These are all symptoms of a nation in which the emphasis upon "character" has declined.

For America to remain a symbol of greatness around the globe, the character of its people is of utmost importance. Hopefully, the lessons from Uncle James can guide us to that place where skin color doesn't matter, but character does.